Holistic Healing

Holistic Healing
Through Channelled Ancients

Channelled by Lucy Dumouchelle
Through the Ancients, Master Twag,
Quan Yin, Hu Li, Dr. Singh

Channelled by Lucy Dumouchelle through the Ancients:
Master Twag, Quan Yin, Hu Li and Dr. Singh.

Copyright© 2012 by Lucy Dumouchelle

All rights reserved. This book may not be reproduced in whole or in part,
stored in a retrieval system, or transmitted in any form or by any means,
electronic, mechanical or other, without written permission
from the publisher, except by a reviewer,
who may quote brief passages in a review.

*Disclaimer: If you have any specific questions about any medical matter,
you should consult a professional healthcare provider.*

Publisher: Mountaintop Healing Publishing, Inc.
P.O. Box 193
Lantzville, B. C.
Canada
V0R 2H0

email inquiries: mountaintophealingpublishing@shaw.ca

First Edition Print version
ISBN: 0987935550
ISBN-13: 978-0-9879355-5-7

Imprints: Mountaintop Healing Publishing Inc

Front cover, "Ancient Energy", original artwork by Tara Cook
Back cover, "Centuries of Age", original artwork by Tara Cook

Dedication

Man's existence has always been torn between war and peace.
Soul, these volumes give an agenda separate from.
The agenda is the healing of mankind.
It is the aim of each individual to be as well as they may be.
We proclaim unto humanity
that humanity combined requires a mutual agenda.
Not singular.
We place this before you.
The way to heal the spirit will give unto thee all that is necessary.
Reach from your human self unto the Soul of your being
which then may reach into the Spirit of all that is.
For you are merely a fragment of all that is.
This we say unto you.
Gathered together are Souls who have made it possible
that these words might come to be.
They are six.*

*Tara Cook
Joanne Drummond
Lucy Dumouchelle
Kitty Lloyd
Grace Piontkovsky
Roman Piontkovsky

The medium and compilers of the present volume
were under strict instruction to record all transmissions
by mechanical means and not to change any detail
in the transcription without verification
from the source of the message.
This we have done.

Acknowledgment

The compilers gratefully acknowledge the assistance of Marianna Vanderklift in proofreading and transcribing.

Preface

Dear readers,

    Within a sentence there often will be a word capitalized,
yet that same word in another sentence will not be capitalized.
The capitalized word is specific to the Farside,
the uncapitalized word is specific to earth.

    For example, humanity comes to earth armed with Truth.
Capitalized Truth is an attribute of Creator that allows
humanity upon earth to recognize and overcome negativity created by man.
Uncapitalized truth is a reference to earth conceptuality
of the word, truth, a truism.

    An earth plane truth changes as wisdom, knowledge accumulates.
What was truth for you as a child, more than likely changed as you matured.
Capitalized Truth does not change, remains always true.

Footnotes are explanations given by Farside.

Table of Contents

Dedication	v
Acknowledgment	vi
Preface	vii
Index	xi
Introduction	1
Remedy	19
Mind	21
Healing, Clarity, Depression, Autism, Alzheimer, Stress, Sleep, Instability	
Head	44
Scalp, Headache, Eyes, Ears, Nose, Mouth, Facial, Throat, Neck	
Upper Torso	67
Hands, Arms, Back, Heart, Lungs	
Lower Torso	91
Abdomen, Legs, Feet	
Full Body	125
Skin, Systemic, Exercise, Food, Color Healing	
Emotions	201
Calm, Fear	
Appendix A Daily East Ritual	210
Appendix B Book List	211

Index

CONDITION	PASSAGE	REMEDY
MIND		
Healing		
Addiction	21	Rose Oil, Rosemary Oil
Ailments, Disabilities, Injuries	25	Healing Tones A B C D F G
Feeling Trapped	22	Mudra
Imbalance	18	East Ritual
Sadness	23	Smile, Laugh
Sadness	24	Mudra
Stress	19	Meditation
Stress	20	Pebbles
Clarity		
Anger	31	Mudra
Anxiety	27	Mudra
Hearing Voices	30	Yellow to White
Lacking Focus	26	Mudra
Lacking Focus	28	Mudra
Tired Mind	29	Mudra
Depression		
Deep Depression, Deep Grief	41	Blue - Madonna
Depression	32	Explanation
Depression	33	Clove Oil
Depression	34	Rose Oil, Rosemary Herb
Depression	35	Phlox Bouquet
Depression	36	Geranium Oil, Olive Oil
Depression	37	Peppermint Tea
Depression	45	Striding

Entering Depression	42	Blue - Medium to Dark
Hopelessness, Futility	44	Coral - Reddish
Mild Depression	40	Green - Mint
Severe Depression	39	Purple
Sore Despair	43	Yellow - Deepest
Stages of Depression	38	Purple - Various Shades

Autism

Autistic and Catatonic - Child	47	Blue - Darker than Eggshell Blue
Description, Fears, Irritants	46	Atmosphere, Diet, Sound

Alzheimer

Agitation	50	Kelp - Dark Green
Anger, Fear	48	Geranium Oil, Macadamia Nut Oil
Jitteriness, Crankiness	49	Pink - Strong

Stress

Anxious	52	Jasmine Oil
Blood Pressure Stress	51	Baking Soda, Olive Oil, Cream of Tartar
Night Terrors	54	Geranium Oil, Macadamia Nut Oil
Panic Attacks, Anxiety, Stress, Worry	53	Geranium Oil, Lavender Oil, Olive Oil
Stress on Body and Mind	55	Verbena - Purple

Sleep

Imbalance	59	Self Hug
Insomniac	58	Mudra
Tension, Stress, Frantic	57	Garlic Oil
Worry	56	Geranium Oil and Diet

Instability

Mental	60	Diet
Schizophrenia	61	Blue - Darker than Eggshell Blue

HEAD

Scalp

Cradle Cap	65	Pine Bark
Dandruff	63	Garlic Oil, Olive Oil
Dermatitis	63	Garlic Oil, Olive Oil
Dry Scalp	62	Cinnamon, Honey, Peppermint Oil, Rose Petals, Rosemary Oil
Eczema	64	Frangipani Flower, Olive Oil
Itching	63	Garlic Oil, Olive Oil
Psoriasis	64	Frangipani Flower, Olive Oil
Psoriasis	62	Cinnamon, Honey, Peppermint Oil, Rose Petals, Rosemary Oil
Scalp Eruptions	64	Frangipani Flower, Olive Oil
Scalp Sores	65	Pine Bark
Sebaceous Cysts	63	Garlic Oil, Olive Oil
Seborrhea	62	Cinnamon, Honey, Peppermint Oil, Rose Petals, Rosemary Oil

Headache

Head Injury, Ache, Sinus	69	Juniper Leaves
Headache - Anxiety	67	Anise Root
Headache - Mild to Severe	68	Salal Leaves, Olive Oil
Headache - Stuffy/Sinus	70	Fireweed Stamen
Headache - Tension	66	Green Beyond Pale
Migraine	71	Position, Pressure, Massage
Migraine	72	Massage, Diet
Migraine	73	Geranium Oil, Jasmine Oil, Lavender Oil, Olive Oil
Migraine	74	Acupressure
Migraine	75	Mulberry Leaves
Migraine	76	Honey, Olive Oil

Eyes

Aching, Red, Swollen	77	Mudra
Allergies	81	Banana
Cataracts	80	Kelp - Brown, Sea Salt. Olive Oil
Far Sighted	85	Bergamot Oil
Irritated-Wind, Air, Allergies	82	Salal Leaves, Olive Oil
Itchy, Watery	83	Cucumber or Squash-Zucchini
Macular Degeneration	79	Carrot, Spinach
Macular Degeneration, Blurred Vision	78	Mudra
Near Sighted	86	Cinnamon Oil, Olive Oil
Occularity	84	Milkweed Head

Ears

Earache	88	Phlox Petals, Olive Oil
Earache	89	Strawberry Buds
Earache	90	Oat Grass
Ringing	91	Yellow to White
Wax Buildup	87	Lavender Oil, Olive Oil

Nose

Allergies/Congestion	94	Juniper Leaves
Broken Nose/Jaw Area	92	Pansies - Deep Purple
Allergies	95	Catnip Tea

Mouth

Bacteria	101	Strawberry Leaves
Candida	97	Peppermint Leaves
Canker Sore	102	Orange Tree Bark
Cold Sores	104	Vanilla Bean
Cold Sores	105	Holly Bark
Colicky Babe	103	Spearmint Oil, Leaves
Dry Mouth	108	Salal Leaves
Gum Disease	99	Peppermint Tea
Gum Disease	101	Strawberry Leaves

Mouth Disease, Pain	100	Phlox Petals
Mouth Sores	97	Peppermint Leaves
Mouth Sores	99	Peppermint Tea
Mouth Sores	104	Vanilla Bean
Mouth Ulcers	101	Strawberry Leaves
Thrush	96	Wallflower
Thrush	97	Peppermint Leaves
Thrush	98	Holly Bark
Thrush	99	Peppermint Tea
Tongue/Mouth Disease	103	Spearmint Oil, Leaves
Tooth Infection	107	Pine Bark
Tooth Pain	106	Juniper Bark
Tooth Swelling	107	Pine Bark
Ulcers	99	Peppermint Tea
Ulcers	104	Vanilla Bean

Facial

Acne	109	Pansy Petals
Astringent	109	Pansy Petals
Cancer - Brain	112	Anise Seed
Cancer - Eyes	112	Anise Seed
Cancer - Head	112	Anise Seed
Cancer - Mouth	112	Anise Seed
Cancer - Throat	112	Anise Seed
Painful Jaw	111	Mudra
Pores	109	Pansy Petals
Roseola, Rosea	110	Apple Blossom Flower

Throat

Congestion	114	Pansy Petals - All But White, Olive Oil
Cough, Sore Throat	115	Plants - All Purple
Cough - Phlegmish	114	Pansy Petals - All But White, Olive Oil
Croup	115	Plants - All Purple
Goiter	113	Clematis Petals, Deep Purple, Olive Oil

Lungs - Sore, Inflamed	115	Plants - All Purple
Nasal Drip	114	Pansy Petals - All But White, Olive Oil
Phlegm	117	Pine Bark
Phlegm	118	Orange, Cayenne Spice, Diet
Phlegm - Cold, Allergies	116	Cedar - Brown Needles
Phlegm In Throat	119	Evening Primrose Leaves
Throat Cancer	113	Clematis Petals, Deep Purple, Olive Oil

Neck

Break - Neck or Spine	121	Pansies - Blue and Purple
Stress and Strain	120	Mudra
Stress, Tension - Pain	122	Beeswax
Tension	123	Exercise

UPPER TORSO

Hands

Arthritic	126	Geranium Oil, Lavender Oil, Rosemary Needles and Rosemary Flowers
Broken Fingers	124	Pansy Flower - Yellow, Salt
Carpal Tunnel	128	Geranium Oil, Lavender Oil, Rosemary Oil
Carpal Tunnel	129	Dry Mustard, Lavender Oil, Rosemary Oil, Olive Oil
Carpal Tunnel	130	Mudra
Rheumatoid Arthritis	127	Banana Peel
Sore	125	Geranium Oil, Lavender Oil, Rosemary Needles

Arms

Arm Pain	132	Eucalyptus Oil, Geranium Oil, Lavender Oil, Rosemary Oil, Olive Oil

Muscles	133	Peppermint Oil. Olive Oil
Ulna Break	131	Pansy Flowers - Yellow, Salt

Back

Arthritic Pain	135	Pressure Point Massage
Arthritic Pain	136	Sedum – Yellow, Olive Oil
Back Pain	143	Massage
Back Weakness	145	Mudra
Back, Lower Weakness	144	Mudra
Backache, Slight Injury	140	Peppermint Oil, Olive Oil
Limb, Neck, Back, Hip Pain	136	Sedum – Yellow, Olive Oil
Osteoporosis	134	Silica
Pain and Stiffness	142	Mudra
Rheumatoid Pain	136	Sedum – Yellow, Olive Oil
Shoulder Injury	141	Mudra
Spinal Corridor	139	Mudra
Spinal Injury	137	Juniper Branch
Spinal Injury	138	Eucalyptus Oil, Geranium Oil, Olive Oil
Spinal Injury Pain	136	Sedum – Yellow, Olive Oil

Heart

Clogged Arteries	146	Rosemary Ground Fresh, Saffron , Olive Oil
Heart Attack	148	Diet, Life Style
Heart Problems	147	Goji Berries
Heart Problems	149	Diet
Palpitations	151	Iris Whole Head - Purple
Palpitations	152	Mudra
Stroke	150	Iris Bud, Olive Oil

Lungs

Bronchial Infections	159	Baobab Fruit
Bronchitis	158	Breathing Exercise, East Ritual, Eucalyptus Oil, Geranium Oil, Olive Oil
Congestion	160	Juniper Leaves
Congestion	161	Shouting
Cough - Croupy	164	Onion Slice
Cough - Dry, Persistent	162	Evening Primrose Leaves, Olive Oil
Cough - Rattling	163	Eucalyptus Oil, Lavender Oil, Rosemary Needles- Fresh
Cough - Soreness	165	Apple Blossom Petals, Rosemary
Croup	159	Baobab Fruit
Lung Congestion	156	Spider Plant - Sprig
Lung Disease	153	Yellow - Light
Lung Disease	154	Sedum Flower - Brown, Olive Oil
Lung Disease	157	Peppermint Leaves
Lung Disease	159	Baobab Fruit
Pneumonia - Walking	155	Eucalyptus Oil, Geranium Oil, Lavender Oil, Rosemary Oil, Mustard - Prepared, Olive Oil
Ribs - Broken	166	Pansy Flowers - Yellow and Purple, Salt
Shortness of Breath	156	Spider Plant - Sprig
Whooping Cough	159	Baobab Fruit

LOWER TORSO

Abdomen

Absorption Difficulty	204	Anise Petals
Bladder Infection	209	Cranberry
Celiac	204	Anise Petals

Celiac, Crohn's	190	Spearmint Leaf
Colic	184	Cinnamon Oil
Colic	188	Spearmint Leaves
Colic	189	Green Tea Leaves
Colic - Colon Area Disease, Gastritis	197	Dandelion Core
Colic - Cramping	185	Wallflower Petals
Colic - Cramps, Diarrhea	183	Amaranth Root
Colic - Diarrhea, Dysentery, Malaria	200	Dahlia Bulb
Colic - Diarrhea, Flu, Grippe	187	Orange Tree Bark
Colic - Gastritis	186	Red Cabbage, Cauliflower
Colitis - Ulcerative	194	Peppermint Oil
Constipation	206	Spearmint Leaves
Constipation	207	Burdock, Diet, Chamomile, Peppermint
Constipation	208	Green Tea, Plumeria Stamen
Cramps	199	Spearmint Leaves
Crohn's	191	Diet, Exercise, Oregano Leaves
Crohn's - Heartburn	192	Lily Pollen - Golden Orange or White
Diaper Rash	203	Marigold Petals - Yellow
Diarrhea	202	Honey, Pine Cone
Digestion	171	Peppermint Leaf
Digestive - Debilitating	175	Periwinkle Leaves
Digestive Problems	172	Peppermint Leaves
Duodenum Ulcer	204	Anise Petals
Dysentery	201	Clover Bud and Leaves, Honey, Rosemary Oil
Gastric - Children	180	Salal Leaves, Olive Oil
Gastritis	196	Rose Petals - Yellow
Genital Warts, Eruptions - Irritated	216	Juniper Bark, Olive Oil
Indigestion	176	Plantain Fruit

Indigestion	177	Peppermint Leaf
Indigestion	179	Mudra
Indigestion	181	Beeswax
Indigestion	182	Squash Skin - Dark Green, Lavender Oil, Olive Oil, Rosemary Oil
Indigestion - Improving	178	Honey
Indigestion - Severe	174	Apple Blossom Petals, Rosemary - Ground
Internal Upset	196	Rose Petals - Yellow
Intestinal Ailments	198	Parsley Sprig
Intestinal Problems	193	Evening Primrose Flower Bud
Kidney Disorder	211	Cranberry, Peppermint Tea
Liver Disease	213	Anise Leaf, Rosemary Needles, Rosemary Oil, Diet, Exercise Oxblood (color)
Liver Disease	214	Anise Leaf
Minor Bladder Infection	210	Mudra
Overeating	173	Clover
Parasites	212	Gardenia Leaf
Pregnancy	167	Geranium Oil, Rosemary Oil, Olive Oil
Pregnancy - 5th Month	169	Banana Peel
Pregnancy - Post	170	Pansy Stem
Pregnancy - Sleep Problems	168	Honey, Marjoram -Powder
Stomach Cancer	215	Periwinkle Leaf
Ulcer - Stress	205	Red Cabbage, Cauliflower Leaves, Olive Oil
Ulcerative Esophagus, Stomach Lining, Colitis	195	Cornflower Petals

Legs

Foot - Break	225	Pansy - Darker Blue
Hip - Arthritis	226	Vegetables - Dark Green, Beta Carotene
Hip - Arthritis/Rheumatism	227	Peppermint Oil, Olive Oil
Hip - Rheumatism	226	Vegetables - Dark Green, Beta Carotene
Knee - Break	225	Pansy - Darker Blue
Knees - Pain	217	Bergamot Oil, Olive Oil, Massage
Leg Aches	221	Ginger Oil, Olive Oil
Leg Stiffness	219	Exercise/Stretch
Leg, Lower - Break	225	Pansy - Darker Blue
Misaligned Discs	226	Vegetables - Dark Green, Beta Carotene
Restless Leg	223	Salt Bath
Restless Leg	224	Green - Medium (color)
Running Injury	228	Geranium Oil, Lavender Oil, Rosemary Oil, Olive Oil
Shin Splints	220	Exercise, Lavender Oil, Olive Oil
Stress/Strain/Varicose Veins	222	Lavender/Violet - color
Thighs - Pain	218	Eucalyptus Oil, Olive Oil, Massage
Varicose Veins	222	Lavender/Violet - color

Feet

Athletes Foot	232	Dandelion Petals, Olive Oil
Athlete's Foot	231	Pansy Leaves, Olive Oil
Bacteria	229	Tansy Leaves
Bunions	245	Baking Soda, Honey, Olive Oil
Burning Feet	239	Peppermint Oil, Olive Oil

Burning/Numb	240	Lavender Oil
Burning Feet - Circulatory	242	Peppermint Tea
Burning Feet - Parkinson's	242	Peppermint Tea
Burning Feet - Restless Leg	242	Peppermint Tea
Carbuncle	231	Pansy Leaves, Olive Oil
Carbuncle	235	Diet
Dry, Cracked Feet	246	White Onion
Feet, Health	230	Olive Oil
Foot Fungus	233	Cedar - Brown Needles
Foot Itch, Burning, Open Sores	236	Honey, Olive Oil
Foot Itching - Diabetic	234	Iris Flower Head- Purple
Fungus	234	Iris Flower Head- Purple
Fungus	235	Diet
Rash	235	Diet
Soreness, Heat	238	Lavender Oil, Peppermint Oil, Olive Oil
Tired & Aching - Walking	242	Peppermint Leaf Tea
Tired & Aching Feet	243	Blackberries
Tired & Aching Feet	244	Geranium Oil, Lavender Oil, Rosemary Needles
Tired, Aching, Burning	237	Lavender Oil, Olive Oil Rosemary - Ground,
Tired, Strain, Pain	241	Lavender or Violet Leaves

FULL BODY
Skin

Acne	270	Macadamia Nut Oil, Rosemary Oil
Acne	271	Geranium Petals
Acne	272	Iris Petals
Acne	273	Red Cabbage, Cauliflower
Acne	274	Daisy Leaves
Acne	275	Banana Peel, Geranium Oil, Olive Oil

Allergic Reaction	249	Rosemary Oil, Sweet Potato, Olive Oil, Diet
Bacteria - Antiseptic Rinse	252	Goji Berry
Blisters	293	Wallflower Leaves
Boils	262	Juniper Leaves
Burns	267	Green Tea
Burns - First And Second Degree	264	Red Cabbage, Cauliflower, Olive Oil
Burns - First Degree	263	Iris Petals
Burns - First Degree	268	Fireweed Stem, Olive Oil
Burns - Second And Third Degree	265	Marigold Petals - Bright Yellow, Olive Oil
Chapped Skin	296	Lavender Oil, Macadamia Nut Oil
Deep Infections	254	Fuchsia Flower
Disease of Muscles - Parkinson's	248	Barberry
Dry Skin	289	Plantain Fruit, Olive Oil
Dry Skin	300	Daffodil Stem
Eczema	249	Rosemary Oil, Sweet Potato, Olive Oil, Diet
Eczema	268	Fireweed Stem, Olive Oil
Eczema	278	Strawberry Leaves
Eczema	279	Strawberry Bud
Eczema	280	Spearmint Leaves
Eczema	281	Juniper Bark, Olive Oil
Electrical Burns	269	Fireweed Root, Olive Oil
Emollient	291	Peony Leaves
Eruptions, Burning, Weeping	288	Barberry Juice, Olive Oil Bergamot Oil, Lavender Oil,
Eruptions, Itching	285	Beeswax, Bergamot Oil, Jasmine Oil, Peppermint Oil, Olive Oil
Festering Sores	259	Liptodorius Leaves
Fungus Infection	255	Garlic Oil, Olive Oil

Herpes - Burning & Soreness	250	Frangipani Flower, Olive Oil
Hives	249	Rosemary Oil, Sweet Potato, Olive Oil, Diet
Lactating/Sore Breasts	295	Lavender Oil, Macadamia Nut Oil
Leprosy	301	Kelp Bulb- Dark Green
Open Wounds, Sores	252	Goji Berry
Poison Ivy	283	Lily Leaves - Deep Orange, Golden Orange or White
Poison Ivy	294	Cayenne Pepper
Poison Nettle	283	Lily Leaves - Deep Orange, Golden Orange or White
Poison Oak	294	Cayenne Pepper
Poison Sumac	283	Lily Leaves - Deep Orange, Golden Orange or White
Psoriasis	249	Rosemary Oil, Sweet Potato, Olive Oil, Diet
Psoriasis	279	Strawberry Bud
Rash - Diaper	287	Strawberry Leaves
Rash - Itchy	286	Clematis Petals - Deep Purple, Olive Oil
Rashes	277	Chamomile Tea, Vitamin E Oil
Roseola	276	Clematis Petals- Deep Purple, Olive Oil
Scabies	249	Rosemary Oil, Sweet Potato, Olive Oil, Diet
Scabies, Bacterial, Insects	284	Red Cabbage, Cauliflower
Scars	261	Garlic Clove, Vitamin E
Severe Trauma	247	Vanilla Liquid, Olive Oil
Skin Eruptions	266	Kelp - Dark Green
Skin Lotion - Sun	282	Kelp Bulb - Dark Green
Sores, Not Infected	261	Garlic Clove, Vitamin E

Sun/Wind Burn Protection	292	Primrose Petals
Sunburn	266	Kelp - Dark Green
Sunburn	269	Fireweed Root, Olive Oil
Sunburn, Sores	290	Mud, Sedge Clippings
Suppurated Wounds	253	Periwinkle Roots
Warts	297	Rosemary Oil, Baking Soda, Olive Oil
Warts	298	Lily Petals - Deep Orange, Golden Orange or White
Warts	299	Liptodorius Flower, Olive Oil
Weeping Sores	258	Vanilla Bean
Wound	251	Salal Leaves
Wounds - Open	256	Oatmeal
Wounds - Open	257	Rye Grass
Wounds, Abrasions, Scrapes	268	Fireweed Stem, Olive Oil
Wounds, Scrapes	260	Marigold Petals - Bright Yellow

Systemic

Aches And Pains - General	361	Baking Soda, Cream of Tartar, Honey, Lemon
Aches, Pains	355	Bergamot Oil, Eucalyptus Oil, Peppermint Oil, Massage
AIDS	306	Holly Leaves
AIDS - Cancer Of The Blood	328	Sedum Florets - Pink
Ailments Affecting Hands/Feet	343	Daffodil Leaves
Air - Toxic	308	Palm Tree, Philodendron, Spider Plant, Maple
Allergy	309	Remove Carpets
Allergy	310	Seaweed Algae
ALS	305	Daffodil Flower

Arthritic & Rheumatoid Arthritis	313	Pine Oil
Bacteria	315	Lavender Oil, Olive Oil
Balance - Out Of	316	Olive Oil
Boils	318	Rose Leaves, Honey
Boils - Young Babies	319	Frangipani Flower, Olive Oil
Bursitis	321	Dandelion Petals, Olive Oil
Calm - Over Active Children	325	Sound and Light
Calm - Nerves	324	Rose Petals (Wild)
Calm - Stress	323	Exercise
Cancer	326	Camomile Oil, Geranium Oil, Lavender Oil, Rosemary Oil, Olive Oil
Cancer - Skin - Tumours	327	Daisy Petals
Candida, Yeast Infection	322	Holly Leaves, Honey
Cannabis - Drug Withdrawal	302	Heliotrope Petals
Carbuncles	318	Rose Leaves, Honey
Carpal Tunnel	330	Juniper Berries, Olive Oil
Chemotherapy	329	Jasmine Oil
Circulation	331	Massage, Olive Oil
Circulation	332	Juniper Berries, Olive Oil
Cold	343	Daffodil Leaves
Cold Virus	333	Lavender Oil, Rosemary Oil, Mustard - Prepared, Lanolin, Jasmine Oil
Diabetic Nerve Damage	343	Daffodil Leaves
Disease - Last Stages	365	Sound
Dizzy	335	Anise Seeds, Ginger Root, Olive Oil
Drug Withdrawal	302	Heliotrope Petals
Drug Withdrawal - Prescription	303	Anise, Water
Drugs - Toxin Release	304	Mudra

Dry Skin - Extreme	336	Apple Blossom
Dystrophy	305	Daffodil Flower
Emotions - Suppressed	337	Release
Energy Imbalance	338	Meditation
Fever	340	Apple Blossom
Fever	342	Vanilla Liquid
Fever - Very High	341	Wallflower Root
Flu	315	Lavender Oil, Olive Oil
Headaches	305	Daffodil Flower
Heroin - Drug Withdrawal	302	Heliotrope Petals
Herpes Sores	345	Phlox Petal Stem, Olive Oil
Hormonal Imbalance	356	Cinnamon Bark
Illness	344	Laughter
Immune Deficiency Sores	307	Holly Bark
Infections	346	Fireweed Petals
Inflammation	311	Tansy Leaf Tea
Influenza	348	Pine Bark
Leprosy	350	Strawberry Leaves
Leprosy - Numb Hands/Feet	351	Clematis Petals - Deep Purple, Olive Oil
Leprosy - Skin	353	Green Tea
Leprosy - Skin Tonic	352	Phlox Stem
Lost Limb Phantom Pain	360	Sedum Florets- Pink. Olive Oil
Lymphatic System Imbalance	354	Mudra
Menopause	356	Cinnamon Bark
Mescal - Drug Withdrawal	302	Heliotrope Petals
Mood Swings, Temperature	356	Cinnamon Bark
Stress, Muscle Strain	330	Juniper Berries, Olive Oil
Nauseous	335	Anise Seeds, Ginger Root, Olive Oil
Nervous System Diseases	357	Geranium Oil, Lavender Oil, Peppermint Oil, Rosemary Oil, Olive Oil
Neuropathy - Nervous System	320	Fireweed Stamen
Parasites - Internal	358	Verbena Root

Parkinson's, Tremors	359	Barberry Berries
Pesticides	304	Mudra
Phlegm	311	Tansy Leaf Tea
Poison	304	Mudra
Posture - Improper	363	Description
Release Toxins	304	Mudra
Restless Sleep - Baby	334	Yellow - color
Restricted Veins/Arteries	305	Daffodil Flower
Rheumatoid Arthritis	312	Pansy Leaves
Rheumatoid Arthritis - Joints	314	Lavender Oil, Rosemary Oil, Baking Soda, Cream of Tartar, Honey, Olive Oil
Sadness/Sorrow/Depression	344	Laughter
Sclerosis	305	Daffodil Flower
Sitting Too Long	339	Exercise
Sleep - Levels	364	Description
Sting - Insect	349	Baobab Leaf
Stroke	305	Daffodil Flower
Swelling/Inflammation	347	Frangipani Flower, Olive Oil
Tendonitis	330	Juniper Berries, Olive Oil
Tobacco Withdrawal	304	Mudra
Tonic - Over 70 Years old	366	Elderberry Wine
Toxic Flush	367	Spearmint Leaves
Vertigo	335	Anise Seeds, Ginger Root, Olive Oil
Virus	315	Lavender Oil, Olive Oil
Wellness - Balance	362	Mudra
Wounds - Small - Antibiotic	317	Rose Root

Exercise

Bedridden, Immobile	373	Lifting Feet
Circulation	370	Wall Exercise
Exercise Benefits	379	Walking
Heart Exercise, Tone	376	Marching
Hip Ache	375	Steps

Lack of Energy - Invigorate	379	Walking
Lack of Exercise	379	Walking
Lack of Tone of Body	368	Marching, Bending, Stretching
Lack of Tone of Mind and Body	369	Waltzing
Reduce Blood Pressure	380	Loping
Relaxing The Tense Body	374	Steps
Sitting At Computer Too Long	372	In Chair Arm Exercises
Sitting Still Too Long	371	In Chair Arm Exercises
Stress	380	Loping
Tense/Tired	378	Mudra
Tension Release	377	Exercises

Food

Alzheimer's	382	Diet
Anemic	391	Garlic Cloves
Caffeine Effects	385	Remove from Diet
Cancer	386	Geranium Oil, Papaya Pulp, Olive Oil
Crohn's	387	Diet
Disaster Areas	388	Purify Water
Flu	390	Garlic Cloves, Olive Oil
Ginseng - Growing	392	Pine Bark, Ginseng Seeds
Grief, Shock	389	Juniper Berries
Illness In Blood	391	Garlic Cloves
Imbalance in Chi	384	Diet, Exercises
Immune System	390	Garlic Cloves, Olive Oil
Itch	393	Bergamot Oil, Geranium Oil, Rosemary Ground, Rosemary Oil, Olive Oil
Lettuce - Altered	394	Warning
Low Energy	383	Amaranth Leaves
Malnutrition	396	Pine Bark
Medicine Chest	395	List
Protein - Lack Of	397	Beetles

Stamina	396	Pine Bark
Toxic Purify	381	Diet

Color Healing

Anxiety In Institutions	405	Brown
Brain Fever	414	Purple
Burn Patients	401	Blue - Madonna
Burn Patients - Lower Extremities	410	Green
Calm Jittery Nerves	413	Pink - Bright
Cancer	409	Green, Chrysoprase, Emerald
Cholera	412	Green - Deep/Dark
Confidence - Lack of	402	Beige
Delirium	416	Purple - Deep
Disability of the Mind	399	Amber
Disease Riddled Elderly	404	Brown
Emotional - Instability	398	Crystals - Yellow and Blue
Fever	414	Purple
Gout	415	Purple
Great Pain	416	Purple - Deep
Grieving Child	403	Brown
Ill Health	417	Red
Insect Diseases for Child	412	Green - Deep/Dark
Lack of Joy	400	Shades of Black - Blue, Greys, Matte Black
Leg Swelling - Leprosy	415	Purple
Leg Swelling - Water Retention	415	Purple
Mental Incapacities of Aged	416	Purple - Deep
Multiple Sclerosis	413	Pink - Bright
Needing Clarity of Mind and Body	418	Yellow
Plague	412	Green - Deep/Dark
Sea Sickness/Altitude Sickness	408	Brown With A Tinge Of Red
Shut out Emotions	400	Shades of Black - Blue, Matte Black, Greys

Spinal Injuries	406	Black/Brown
Spirituality	400	Shades of Black - Blue, Matte Black, Greys
Tension/Stress - Release	402	Beige
Terminal Patients	411	Green
Violent Mentality	407	Brown With A Tinge Of Red

EMOTIONS
Calm

Addictive Personality	419	Camomile Tea, Lavender Oil, Lavender - Color
Agitation, Anger, Anxiety	429	Rocking
Agitations of the Mind, Alzheimer's	420	Kelp - Dark Green
Alzheimer's	422	Exercise
Angst and Anger - Alzheimer's	421	Dandelion Stalk
Bed of the Ill	424	Evening Primrose Petals
Calm The Mind - Refocus The Cells	426	Blue - Deep Indigo
Coma	422	Exercise
Crying Child - Soothing	425	Blue - Eggshell/Madonna
Emotional Turmoil	429	Rocking
Fever	422	Exercise
Final Stages of Illness	423	Rose Oil
Nations at War	432	Blue - Madonna
Panic and Anxiety Attacks	431	Jasmine Oil
Pregnancy - First Stages	428	Peppermint Oil
Reducing Pain Medications	429	Rocking
Stress	427	Beeswax
Troubled in Mind and Body	422	Exercise
Wells of Sorrow and Pain	430	Frangipani Aroma

Fear

Anger	435	Acceptance
Anger	436	Kidney Cleanse

Anxiety	436	Acceptance
Fear	433	Purple - Light
Fear of Unknown - Children	434	Mudra
Holding Fear	437	Mudra
Negative Emotionality	436	Kidney Cleanse
Restless Sleep	438	Life Acceptance
Worry	435	Acceptance
Worry	439	Compassionate Mode

Introduction

1   We would give you some of our history.
It is Truth we spent much time in the land you call India, Pakistan,
    for we spent much time on what is now the border between the two.
But we also traveled extensively throughout all of Asia
    and into even parts of what you call Europe.
And we were apprentice for twenty three years
    to a herbalist who taught us much.
And then as we dedicated the rest of our life
    to assisting and helping others with our knowledge,
    we entered in to what you term channelling,
    and received from the Farside[1] teachers
    a more extensive library of knowledge.
This is combined with other healers, other herbalists.
And many times, that is why we say we are of.
For although we have named ourselves for earth identification.
    and although our Spirit is primary within this medium,
    there are a multitude of others who participate also,
    from time to time as channelled entities.
From many different worlds are we.
And all have been upon the earth, in one incarnation or another.
Some of us in many incarnations,
    for we had a streak of stubbornness
    and we needed to enter in time and time again
    in order to learn our chosen lessons.
We would have you understand,
    that in the life within the India, Pakistan area,
    the forty two years were spent outside a hut
    built of all natural materials
    and placed against the mountainside,
    where we had our little bowls of various herbs, flowers, seeds, oils.
And where we sat in the lotus position and advised and offered advice
    to those who came seeking healing, and none were ever refused.
Food was provided by the generosity of the villagers nearby.

---

1 Farside - the Path unto Creator Energy, known as heaven.

Song and comradeship was also provided by these generous people
    and later by those who called themselves student
    and who built a compound to live close by the teacher.

2   Soul, we come before you to place answers to questions.
Indeed, the information we have given
    and will give is available to all who may access.
Souls of earth, we have intent of being, of being within your space,
    of bringing unto you what little knowledge we have accumulated
    through our many lifetimes, not only within your earth plane
    but also of the many adventures upon the Farside.
We have many levels of existence.
We have many planes of being.
We have learned wisdom.
We have spent lifetimes learning to accept the wonder of our being.
We have spent many lifetimes indulging in all forms of negativity
    and we have spent lifetime upon lifetime overcoming that negativity,
    and reaching unto the self, the sacred self of our being.
We spoke many times with the resonant radiance of Angels,
    of learned beings, beings who had wisdom
    and ultimate knowledge of herbs and various efficacious remedies
    to assist in the healing of a tortured Soul,
    of a being in pain, of a being in emotional distress.
We count ourselves as privileged to be able to enter in,
    and to entertain your being in teachings of modalities of healing.
We have only intent to bring forth
    that which will ease your placement upon the plane of earth
    in as much as your Soul will allow.
Energy, healing with Energy is of the utmost efficacity.
And so we offer to you modalities that are natural,
    that are not manmade, that instead
    are made from that which Creator has gifted unto thee,
    are made with the Spirits of beings who have offered themselves
    to help humanity; those flowers, those herbs, shrubs,
    all manner and parts of trees.
These beloved herbs and plants have freely and
    willingly entered in for earth, for mankind.
For they have conscious awareness and willingly, even gladly,
    give their being unto the sustenance and maintenance of mankind.

HOLISTIC HEALING

Souls of earth, you have upon your planet,
> wood in many guises,
> from the very smallest of twigs to the very giants of trees.

And we would have you understand that all wood has healing properties.
Each wood stands ready to enter in to healing vibration for an individual.
Much of your medicines are derived from trees, from wood.
Understand that the medicines, the remedies
> that are derived from trees are freely given unto mankind
> and understand it is the vibration of the tree that is the stimulus
> in the healing properties of the remedy.

It is the vibration of the tree that may heal the facial structure,
> the jaw pain, the toothache, the cheek bones broken,
> the furrowed brow; the elm is particularly efficacious.

You will understand that for the spinal area the baobab tree
> is especially efficacious.

You will understand that for the internal organs it is the juniper.
For the external torso of the body it is the cedar.
For the lower portion of the body from the hips on down it is the pine tree.
For the feet, it is the bamboo.
Understand, we speak of all the relations,
> the many names, the genus of these trees.

In some cases, it is the sap,
> in many cases it is the bark.

You need not, Soul, destroy, maim the tree.
It will willingly share its vibration in its bark, in its sap.

3   We would bring unto you this day further knowledge
> of the plant life that exists upon your planet.

You understand that each plant has within a particle of wellness
> and also the potential when used extensively to be harmful.

It is imperative that you recognize, when we give amounts,
> they are given so that only the goodness is prevalent.

Using more than the amount given will not speed the process.
You will not become well quicker.
You will not stop itching faster.
But you may overwhelm your body with too much.
We ask that you follow the amounts given,
> the directions given, as they were given.

We would ask that you recognize
> that all plant life has Soul, has offered itself to assist mankind.

We have a great reverence for these plants.
Be aware of their ability
    to assist you in your earth path.
The great trees of earth and when we say great trees,
    we speak even of the small bush, of the small twig.
All that is woody is a great tree,
    is magnificent in its ability to assist mankind.
Souls of earth, have a care for your earth, for that which grows.
For as you destroy species, you destroy the potential of that species
    to assist you in your wellness and in your walk.

4 We would have you understand,
    there are differences that occur in chemical compositions
    between powdered, between dried, and between fresh.
It is, Souls of earth, imperative for the efficacy of the remedy
    to follow the directions for dried, fresh, or powdered.
It is within the body itself, the particular state of the enzymes,
    that decide whether one is to use powdered, dried, or fresh.
It has to do with the chemical reaction of the body and the disease.
The beings will understand that to be fully efficacious
    the remedies given, the instructions given, must be done together.
A partial will not suffice.
Heed for full efficacy all instructions.
Whether they be for time[2], for amount, for combination.
And whether it be exercise or food or herb,
    they are to be done in conjunction for full efficacy.
For it is often the combination that is required
    for the full healing to occur.
A full healing always is optimal for each being.
But we would caution
    that if you are selective in taking bits and pieces of a remedy,
    it will not be efficacious.
The book will be sorted by body parts.
And so it will be with the rest of the body.
In many cases, there will be more than one body part
    and so it will appear therefore in the various body parts.
The treatment in general form, Soul, has benefit
    but not in a case where the being resists.

---

2 time - in all cases, unless otherwise specified, times are in seconds.

The mind, Soul, is strong.
The brain has been encapsulated for many years
    with certain arguments for medical treatments.
This happens often upon your earth plane.
There is an authority given, an air of authority given,
    that often people succumb to.
Soul, we would offer an alternative and it is up to the being to decide.
This may be done at the same time as the medical treatment
    if the being is more comfortable to do so.

5   We would have you understand
    the proclivity of many beings upon your earth
    to entertain within their beings viruses
    that can mutate and become a detrimental,
    anathemic[3] to the health and well being of an individual.
Viruses are part and parcel of nature,
    and you have within you natural immunities
    to many viruses, to many germs.
But, we would have you understand,
    the natural immunity that you have
    is preconditioned upon a balance, upon wellness of being.
When your body and mind is in balance,
    your natural immunities are operating fully.
When you are in imbalance, either in mind or body,
    you decimate your natural immunities and are therefore open to,
    and have a proclivity for, the detrimental effects of a virus.
All upon your earth has reason for existence,
    and all in their natural state of wellness has balance.
Understand the importance
    of having a positive mind and body balance.
It does not become a matter of concern
    if you have what humankind looks at as a disability,
    for you may still be in balance, mind and body,
    you may still be in wellness with a disability.
It is not that which causes the imbalance.
What causes the imbalance
    is your proclivity for tension and stress,

---

3 anathemic - compromising the immune system.

and for the body it is your proclivity for processed foods
   that causes a great deal of imbalance.
Harken, Souls of earth, to balance of mind and body,
   and know when you are in balance you have a natural immunity
   to the great majority of viruses of the earth.
So we urge you to balance your being, mind and body,
   in wellness and in positive growth.

6   We would have you understand the mind
   and the Soul and the body are not separate.
They form a working relationship
   in the daily battles with negativity.
We would address to you the human body's capabilities.
You have a complex mechanism that you call body.
Indeed it is a miraculous organ.
Your bodies have the ability,
   when in tune with the mind, to control the body temperature.
You may heat up your body, the temperature, and you may cool it down.
You do not only because you refuse to accept that you can.
Souls of earth, your body is limitless in its possibilities of healing.
There is not one iota of a disease, illness, emotional upset,
   mental aberration, that you can not heal,
   when the mind, the body and the Soul
   acknowledge their connection.
Operating individually, there are problems.
For the mind to sever, to isolate self from Soul,
   casts a pall of darkness around the being.
For the mind to isolate itself from the body causes fear
   to the body; pains, illnesses, destruction of limbs.
We encourage the recognition
   of the connection of mind, body and Soul.
If you would reach for all your possibilities,
   all you need to do is accept that connection,
   and that operating within this Holy triad
   will bring forth healing, not only for self but for others.

7   The choice becomes to understand your being is in wellness
   and not allow the various irritations to become you.
That is the trap,
   it is to focus in on those irritations, to become those irritations.

Mankind, understand all that you see as illness,
    all that you see as plagues upon your being
    are opportunities to overcome.
You are all spiritual beings.
You are more than your earth self.
To focus on your dilemmas detracts from the healing process.
To enter in to life, to enter in to joy is to know you are in wellness.
True healing has a myriad of definitions.
True healing to earth may simply be the ability to go through life
    without illness or incapacity of any kind.
True healing may be the bent hand is suddenly no longer bent.
True healing is not in the eyes of the beholder,
    for you do not know what a person agreed to in a lifetime.
They may have agreed to come with an incapacity.
They may have agreed to come with an illness,
    not only for their own growth but as a teacher to others
    and for the growth of others or to pay karma.
True healing is a misnomer.
We call it, to be in wellness.
In wellness the spirit rests within the being.
In wellness there is Love.
In wellness there is no judgment.
In wellness, even though the physical body may be incapacitated,
    it matters not, for you follow your path.
Beloved Souls of earth,
    we would have you know, the raucous intent that occurs
    when the body is in need of healing, of balance,
    of intention, of purpose, of well being.
Your bodies are magnificent works of artistry.
They are incredibly complex and yet simple in their aim to be in balance.
And in order for wellness,
    in order for well being to be a part of your existence,
    balance of heart, mind, body and Soul is a requirement.
We would have you understand, we offer
    and it is then your choice to accept.
We offer unto you a plate, not empty, but full of joy.
Will you accept, Soul?
Will you partake of this plate of joy?
Indeed, you would find your days will be productive
    if you partake each day of joy.

Find those moments of joy.
Whether it be in the most minute; looking at a sea shell,
> immersing yourself in the construction of the seashell,
> and for those few moments, focusing on the wonder.
This is a joyous moment, indulge in it.
Find it in your day moments of joy,
> whether simple or complex is irrelevant.
It is the finding of the moment that is important.
We would have you consider looking at your life,
> the many years that are left, as the fountain.
The fountain gurgles happily, moves in and out, in and out.
And we would have you look at your life as merely an
> entering in and an entering out each day.
And that all that you do in the glory of your being is a gift,
> not only to Creator, but to mankind.
You are not alone in this.
All of humanity gives a gift to both their Creator and mankind.
Do not indulge in perspicacity of depression.
Find those moments of joy and be as the fountain.
Accepting, accepting, accepting.[4]
So be it.

8 All Souls may absorb healing and will process as required.
Each being has a free will and choice.
You may offer healing to anyone but they have not to accept it.
There are many reasons for that.
They may be teaching another being.
They may be an example for another being
> or it may simply be their walk to carry that ailment,
> to experience the debilitation.
The reasons are myriad.
Send forth your healing in pure Love and compassion.
The acceptance is up to the other.
Enter in, Soul.
Allow the vibration to expand throughout your being.
Enter beyond the earth.
Reach for the holiness of your Soul.

---

4 accept - to be in a state of knowing all is a lesson
and has reason for being.

The most effective,
   the most efficacious form of healing
   is connect to your sacred self from the Farside,
   healing with the pure Love of your Creator.
And that healing is open unto all without exception.
But you must release negative
   so that you may connect with the sacred self.
We offer this knowledge with Love and compassion.

9 We would have you understand
   the imbalance within your whole being.
You will understand the need to refrain foods
   that have no food value,
   that contain little to no nutrition for your being.
For they take up the space of that
   which would be nutritious for your being,
   specifically those items fried with oils,
   those items containing much salt,
   those items that contain much sugar of white or brown
   or contain sweeteners.
Imbibing this type of food, you in essence begin
   to starve your system of nutrients that are necessary for wholeness,
   for wellness, for balance.
We would have all of earth understand,
   the body in its complexity is simplistic in its need for wellness.
Upon your earth was given a proliferation of fruits and vegetables,
   legumes and nuts.
Less was given of meats and grains.
A diet heavy in fruits and vegetables, legumes, light in flesh
   and light in grains is a body in balance and wellness.
All that you require may be found in the balance diet as we have given.
Soul, we have suggested very little processed foods.
Not only those you find in your markets,
   but those that are processed within your home.
For heat affects food and changes the chemical composition.
To get the most nutritive value,
   it is best to not submit the food to great degrees of heat.
A light steaming where steaming is acceptable.
All foods that are vegetable should indeed be raw.
You will not, Soul, involve yourself in the ingestion of raw meats.

For even a fish raw is dangerous for the amount of pesticides within.
We would ask that you limit the amount of food that needs to be cooked.
We would suggest that you concentrate
>   your protein intake with that of nuts and legume,
>   for they do not require great processing,
>   and limit all other processing.

10 We would discourse with you on sugar.
Sugar, when nutrients have been removed,
>   has no value for the human flesh, blood, mind.

Indeed, an excess of sugar in its refined chemicalized state
>   is detrimental to the well being,
>   to the health of the flesh, of the mind.

With the ingestion of a refined sugar, whether it be white,
>   yellow, or brown,
>   the body must work overtime in an attempt to digest it
>   and to still its effects upon the system of the mind.

Mankind was given sugar, was given sweetness in its pure state.
In its pure state
>   there are nutrients that will enhance the physical brain and body.

We would have you understand the havoc
>   refined sugar plays upon the human body.

Man has taken the natural benefit, the nutrient,
>   and refined it to a state of non existence,
>   whereupon one is left only with the sweetness,
>   not with the goodness inherent in many sugars.

We ask that you be aware that as you enter in to your body
>   refined foods, although filling,
>   they lack the basic nutrients required for optimal wellness of being.

And have not only been reduced in potency,
>   but be aware that the processing involved
>   may bring into your body chemicals and substances
>   not normally found by ingesting the actual plant or sap.

Indeed, Souls of earth, we offer this to you for your awareness.
We do not judge, we do not encourage and we do not prohibit,
>   we only offer for your knowledge.

11 We would speak to Africa, to the land of Africa,
>   to the toxicity of the land that gets into all food stuffs,

that gets into, enters in to all plants,
   that is entering in to the people of Africa.
The land requires scouring.
People, within a generation your children will be born toxic.
You may reverse, but it must be done, Souls of earth, now.
It will take a generation to reverse the toxicity, the pollution of the land,
   for it is within each grain of sand.
There is no pocket of cleanliness left within this great continent.
Lead.
Indeed, Souls, lead.
The source is the mines.
It is necessary to form a chain of goodness around this continent,
   to form a circle of White Light,
   to form a goodness emanating from thousands
   upon thousands of beings,
   to sweep the land, to scour it with the Light.
Beings of earth you have this capability.
You have this power.
You have at your disposal this wonderfully cleansing Light
   placed as a dome over the continent,
   so that the cleansing enters in deep into the land.
And the toxins arise as a miasma, a fog and are dissipated
   by the sun of the Light that you have placed.
Souls of earth, in many parts of the world there is toxicity of the land
   due in many cases to lead,
   but also many other chemical concoctions of man.
But they are not as concentrated as they are in Africa,
   nor have they been in existence
   as long as they have been in this continent.
Africa, Souls of earth, is a place of great learning,
   is a place of great pain, is a place of great humanity and courage.
Look to your children, people of Africa.
Look to the future generation.
Care for them now, before,
   not after when they will litter literally your hospital beds.
Souls of earth, in a twinkling of an eye you may alter this.
We would ask, nay we would plead. with mankind to refrain
   from the continual experiments upon animals
   with growth hormones.

For you are tainting the very Purity of these beings
> and in tainting the Purity of these beings you taint yourselves
> as you ingest the flesh of these beings.

Souls of earth, mankind was given,
> offered the lives of these beings for your nutritional values.

And in their pure state they did, indeed, provide nutrition.
Not that they were the only nutrition, but they were a pure choice with,
> amongst the choice of all the other pure; vegetables, fruit, legumes.

Mankind was not satisfied with the rate of growth given by Creator.
And hence began the experiments to speed the growth
> and this has resulted in mutations
> largely within the community of animals,
> but also now into the community of vegetables
> and into the community of beans, legumes.

Mankind, we ask that you cease experimenting
> upon that which nourishes your being.

Take from nature that which you require
> to sustain your being in health and goodness.

Abstain from that which is tainted.
For the taint brings not only unto thy being illness
> and mutation of your cells, of your genes
> but then that mutation is passed on to your children
> and your children's children.

Souls of earth, pause and think carefully of that which you do.

12 Soul, you will understand heavy metals reside,
> indeed, rebound, through all of earth.

It is that in some places they are more concentrated than in other places
> and it is that some beings are more susceptible than other beings.

By susceptible we mean that they retain within their being more
> than their being can possibly,
> in their current state of ill, disseminate.

Many people, because they are in a state of wellness,
> of high health, may we term it, are able to deal with
> the heavy metals that enter in to their system
> and eventually flush them out through well living.

But there are those who have been weakened, for whatever reason,
> who are then more susceptible to holding within
> and being unable to rid themselves of the heavy metals.

You will understand that mercury is only one of many
  that are possible to be in contact with.
It is, Soul, the idea of the gyro, of always particulates
  moving within the air, particulates gyrating.
And the being suspended within that gyro and absorbing the particulates;
  it is as if arrows were penetrating the body.
We have suggested previously to mankind that the skin is as a sponge
  and absorbs toxicities, pesticides, particulates.
It need not come into the mouth or the lungs to enter in to your body.
You have pores, thousands of pores.
The body is magnificent in its ability to cleanse, to flush toxins,
  but that system, as in any system, may be overwhelmed.
And when it is overwhelmed, generally through stress,
  then illness enters in.
Mankind, we plead with you to understand
  the deleterious effects of stress and toxins upon your being.

13 Understand the vibration of toxic gases,
  materials or liquids have a low vibration.
This is true also for the vibration of negative or toxic energy.
That which you emit, which is negative,
  which is harmful, toxic not only to self
  but to others of mankind and to earth,
  emits a low vibration,
  but a penetrating vibration nonetheless.
You have within both possibilities of
  the low vibration and the high vibration.
Understand, both are created by you, individual,
  both have potential and possibility; the choice is yours.
We would expand upon the effects of negative emotionality
  upon the being, physically and mentally.
Understand, negative emotions affect the inners of your being
  and in their eruptions affect the outers of your being.
When you hold within a negative energy,
  you place stress upon the body's organs.
When you hold within negative energy, you place upon the mind
  a dampening of its ability to function in a logical manner.
And the negative energy is not contained within thy being
  and it expands outward to all beings

whether they be animate or inanimate,
whether they are human or creatures of the earth.
Souls of earth, negative energy does not bring about health
in any sense of the word.
It does not bring about
wellbeing of the body and the mind.
It is simply detrimental and in no way efficacious.
That is not to say that there is no reason for negative energy,
for you are aware of the purpose of humanity.
But, Souls of earth, it is not necessary to hold on to negative energy.
It is not necessary to increase the growth of negativity.
Indeed not.
You will understand that many of your companions,
your cats, your dogs, your birds,
and other creatures within your home environment,
indeed, are also affected negatively by negativity.
And they have no choice to reject it
for they have come to assist mankind,
they freely and willingly and lovingly accept.
That is not to say that you need to share the negative energy.
Indeed not, Souls of earth.
Understand, negative energy is inimical to the wellness of being.
It is that simple.
And yet, within the body and the mind develop great complexities
to overwhelm the simplicities of life.
There is no judgement to this.
There is only a request for awareness of that which you do.
Soul, we would have you understand that drugs,
low dosage or high dosage, in any case affect the body.
They alter the natural flow of the body and place upon it an unnatural stress.
This is often helpful when a bacterium
has altered the whole structure of the body.
In those cases, Soul, indeed the alteration is a positive not a negative effect.
All that enters in to the body, the body must recompense in some way.
It must integrate or spew out that which has entered in.
If it can not, Soul, in its optimum processes,
its optimum manufacturing processes utilize, then it must spew out.
In a normal manufacturing process
the spewing out is done through your kidneys, your liver,
your intestinal system and even through the pores of your skin.

When it is an abnormal process, Souls of earth,
    in the cases of that which alters the system,
    then the body becomes confused
    in how to deal with this foreign substance.
Understand, Souls of earth, that we are in the most basic terminology
    attempting to explain to you
    what happens synergistically within the body.
When you have, Soul, this foreign substance,
    the body does not know how to spew it out,
    for it does not belong in any of its manufacturing processes.
And therefore you erupt in physical,
    physiological symptoms of diseases, ailments, illnesses.
And you have all manner of internal complication
    and external complications that arise.
It is, Souls, as in your manufacturing plants,
    when your machinery is overwhelmed and overworked
    it breaks down and causes a disruption in the process.
So too the manufacturing process within the body.

14 We would have you understand aluminum
    was not to be ingested or absorbed into the human body.
Indeed all things are placed upon the earth for a reason,
    but not all are to be within the human body.
An excess of any metal, be it even iron,
    causes an imbalance within the body.
Any imbalance within the body,
    causes what you call illness or disease,
    and, indeed, stresses the delicate balance of the body.
The human body
    is an incredibly magnificent parameter of healing.
There is constant healing within the body
    to obviate the toxins, the metals that are ingested
    whether by mouth, by air.
For indeed, the skin is as a sponge
    and absorbs all that is around it, all that falls unto it.
Any excess, the body will attempt in its intricate magnificence to adjust.
But it has limits to that which it can do within its physicality.

Aluminum[5] is particularly distressing to the human body.
For it enters in to the pathways of the brain.
And thereby affects the mental capacity of your being.
In effect it is cell destroying.
There are some chemicals that are so inimical to the body,
    that even minute amount becomes overwhelming
    and beyond the processes of the body.
To cleanse the being from aluminum,
    requires a dedicated and intensive therapy.
You may embark upon a program of high protein,
    low fat, no meat, no fish diet.
No sugars of any kind, not even honey for a period of three months.
You will also bathe daily with lavender water even unto the scalp,
    it must enter in to all pores of the being.
The feet will be soaked daily in both the lavender water and comfrey tea.
Immerse the feet and hands entirely
    for a total of fifteen minutes, three times daily.
Also daily indulge in a brain exercise.
Any new learning, any activity,
    that will provide exercise to the mind.
This is to be done for a period of one half hour each day,
    minimum, preferably thrice daily.
The beings are to exercise the body daily,
    twenty minute vigorous walks.
If walks are not possible,
    then twenty minutes of some type of vigorous activity,
    where the blood pumps through the body to the veins
    and enhances the activity of the cells of your body.
Any being in the beginning stages of Alzheimer must also understand,
    they require refraining from all stress.
Much has been given on meditation and stress.
Take that which appeals to thy being, and use it to remain in a calm state.
For your objective is to allow the body to heal
    and stress prohibits that activity.
Massage is also another activity that may be done daily.

---

5 Aluminum - Souls, there is the Alzheimer, Parkinson's,
Muscular Dystrophy. There is the Schizophrenia,
and then we have those diseases that directly affect the intestine,
the cancer of the bowels.

The gentle massage of the spinal column
>   is most efficacious in bringing forth
>   and enhancing that healing of the body.
Massage is done in a circular motion
>   all the way throughout the whole spinal column.
You are, indeed, what you eat.
There is a synergy that takes place with the food, the toxins you ingest,
>   and that which is your body.

15 We would have you understand,
>   the touch of your hands can be positive or negative.
It is your intent that will decide the choice that you make.
Intent is powerful when used with option.
A simple intent, only wishing thought, holds little power.
Intent with use holds great power.
We would have you understand,
>   no judgment is placed by Farside on your choices.
No judgment is placed upon your intent.
No judgment is placed upon the action that resolves.
But we would urge that you use these hands to give aid,
>   to give succor, to soothe,
>   to place loving Energy upon the troubled being,
>   to caress the sobbing child, to comfort the aged and the sorry.
We urge you to use your hands,
>   to prepare food for the hungry, to share that which you have.
This we say unto you.

16 We would speak on emollients.
Throughout your world various emollients are concocted
>   to assist the human body, to assist the flesh, the skin.
We would have you understand, Souls of earth,
>   that many of these emollients that have been traditionally used
>   are anathema to the well being of your body:
Those that have to do with whale,
>   those that have to do with human or animal urine,
>   those that have to do with the waste products of any being,
>   those that have to do with the internal brains of various animals
>   and those that have to do with the inner organs of animals
>   were not to be for the human body.

You have available emollients destined for the human body
    such as your olive oil, your primrose oil, your vitamin oils,
    your oils from nuts, your oils from the coconut,
    oils from plants, flowers.
These may be used to assist the human flesh.
The others cause imbalance, cause disease,
    lead to malnourishment of the flesh they are supposed to help.
Many males upon your earth use these
    unnatural emollients for sexual pleasure.
They have convinced themselves that this will enhance.
They do not understand that it is the mind that is convinced.
It is not the inners that they are using
    that has anything to do with enhanced sexual activity.
Souls of earth, the parts of animals are not meant to be rubbed on the skin.
The inners of animals will not
    contribute to your wellness in any way.
Understand, your flesh is a sensitive organ,
    what you absorb enters in to all the cells of your being.
We remind you of this, to bring to your awareness that which you do.

Remedy[6]

These remedies are arranged sequentially: Mind, Head, Upper Torso, Lower Torso, Full Body, and Emotions.

17 We would speak upon muscles of the human body.
A study of the muscles would convince any being, even the most skeptical,
    of the intricate complexity and of beauty of the Creator.
As the skin is a conductor into your being
    of all that is in the air around your being, the muscles, Soul,
    conduct to your inners wellbeing or disabling.
The two, the outer and the inner, are as a symphony.
When the notes are struck in pureness and in accord
    the symphony swells in beauty, in wellness.
So it is with the human body;
    when in accord, a symphony of wellbeing occurs.
When a portion of a being goes awry,
    there are a myriad of remedies that may be imbibed.
There is upon the earth, within what you call nature,
    all that is required to assist in the healing of any being.
Within what you call nature, we have included exercises
    designed to focus upon a particular part of the body,
    and designed to instill, to ignite
    the natural healing ability of your being.
You will find within these pages, remedies available
    to a particular part of your world;

---

[6] Remedy - We would caution that all information is to be utilized from the flower, from the plant that is without taint of pesticide, herbicide, or growth hormones. All of those chemicals will prevent the efficacity of the remedy.

others, not available in your particular part of the world,
but you will find, Souls of earth, a remedy
that will be in your part of your world, for the same.
Within these pages are also remedies using color and sound.
Color and sound upon your earth,
when placed together, are most efficacious in healing.
You have, Souls of earth, a deep well of healing that you may enter in to,
that you may dip into, that you may touch.
Soul, you will find within the pages many different terminologies
for the acknowledgment and understanding
of a variety of languages.
The olive oil is used to bind, to give a consistency,
but it is also a preventative for further eruptions.
It is a cleanser of the skin and in its permeation of the skin
it enters the body and gives forth,
within the body, healing, preventative remedies.
We can not stress enough on the properties for healing
of olive oil in its pure form.
It is efficacious for man and animal.
It is a form of the Balm of Gilead.

Mind

Healing
18 Will you accept healing, Soul?
Begin a daily ritual of facing east[7] as you arise.
Hands outward, for two minutes,
    you will receive the healing Love of your Creator.
You will feel the Energy enter in.
At the end of the two minutes, you will complete a circle of being[8].
And then placing your hands together
    you will sit for a further fifteen minutes facing east,
      and holding your being so and receive.
Simply allow and accept.

19 A healing meditation.
We would have you lay quietly in a darkened room with a light covering.
We would have you place palms upward.
They may rest on the bed or on your body.
We would have you slightly tilt your head back,
    mouth open and focus on your third eye.
Allow the color purple to enter in to your whole body,
    not to one particular spot, to your whole body.
The color is waiting, you need only draw it in.

---

7   east – see Appendix A

8   complete a circle of being – "At the end of your commune
allow thy being mentally or physically to make a complete circle,
turning to your right, to the south, and then to the west,
then to the north, and back again to the east." The Binary,
<u>The Mend, (Holistic Healing Through Channelled Entities)</u>,

Feel it enter your being, surround your being with Energy of Love,
> Energy of Light and Energy of healing.

Contemplate this Light, this color, for ten minutes, thrice daily
> and know you are healed.

20 We would have you understand the value of pebbles,
> the little rocks.

It will be amazingly soothing to your being.

We would have you understand the pebbles we speak of
> do not need to be completely rounded
> but they do require some roundness.

They need be no bigger than from one half to one and a half
> inches or its equivalent in your centimeters.

You will, Soul, understand they may be any color
> but not sharp edged.

Ideally they are from the ocean,
> but also from the land they will be efficacious.

Those from the land will be dipped in salt water,
> and allowed to sit in the water for at least three minutes,
> and then they may be taken out and used.

After each use they must again be placed back into salt water.

Into the palms of each hand you will place only enough
> that you may close your hand over.

Roll them around in the palm of your hand.

The first rolling around will take place within each palm
> for a period of no more than five seconds.

And then cup your hands and hold them within the cup of both hands.

Rub the pebbles clockwise for no more than twelve seconds.

Even the youngest of a child may indulge in this exercise.

Placing it between the two palms energizes the meridians, the chakras.

This may be done as often as you find it necessary throughout the day.

This may be done in preparation for a deeper meditation.

This may be done in preparation for any activity that causes angst.

This may be done to assist the grieving.

This will also, Soul of earth, help those
> who are in lesser pain to ease their pain.

21 We would address addiction.

The brain has convinced the body that it requires this to exist.

The body in its state of wellness craves nothing.

In chemicals, in what you call narcotics,
    there needs to be compassion during the stage of reversal.
For the mind is screaming, as the body is.
All who are entering in to reversal require the oil of rosemary
    placed upon the third eye and upon the wrist, pulse area.
We would have the oil of rosemary mixed with oil of rose
    and massaged into the palms of the hand and the palms of the feet,
    every two hours and it will assist the being in recovery.

22 We give unto you an exercise for those beings
    caught in the cycle of negativity, feeling unable to break out,
    though they wish it dearly within their hearts.

Step 1
Place your body in a chair.
Sit comfortably, if possible, feet upon the floor.

Step 2
Place your hands flat upon a surface,
    placing the left forefinger over the nail of the right forefinger.
The fingers, except for the forefingers that are touching,
    will be spread apart.
The thumbs will not be touching.

Step 3
Slowly raise your hands upright, upward until
    you reach the level of your earth eyes.

Step 4
At this point, Soul, you will allow
    the pads of your forefingers to come together,
    the pads of the thumbs to come together,
    and let the rest of the fingers fall towards the palm.

Step 5
You will have created a form.
Place that form in front of your earth eyes,
    bringing your hands close until the thumbs touch the nose
    and the forefingers are touching the area of the third eye.
Hold that position for a count of five.

Step 6
Three times, take a deep breath in through the nostrils,
>   hold for the count of three
>   and release that breath slowly to the count of five;
>   concentrating on controlling the exhalation of the breath:
wh, wh, wh, wh, wh.

Step 7
After the third exhalation, move the thumbs and the forefingers,
>   still touching each other, but move it away from your face,
>   and open the other fingers.

Step 8
Slowly bring both hands down back unto the surface.

Step 9
As you reach back unto the surface, you may then
>   separate the thumbs and the forefingers.

Step 10
Place your hands palm upward and feel the vibrational Energy
>   in the area of your earth eyes and your third eye.
And you will know by that feeling of the vibration
>   that you have the exercise in its completeness.
And you will, Soul, break the circle of negativity.

23 We would have you clearly understand the muscles used to smile
>   are connected to what you call endorphins of the mind.
The act of the smile moves the muscles
>   in such a way that it triggers a reaction.
It is why, Souls, even a small smile will lighten another being,
>   for there is an Energy that is emitted
>   because of the reaction to the muscle movement.
And indeed, the wider, the more giving of the smile,
>   the more there is released.
It is no accident, Souls of earth, that laughter brings healing,
>   for laughter done in a positive frame of mental acuity,
>   allows an increase tenfold
>   in the reaction of the muscles and the mind.

We would suggest that as part of your optimum health process,
>   that each day you smile largely, and that you laugh joyfully.

24 The putting the tongue between the teeth, and then
>   blowing air, thffff thffff thffff, three times,
>   you will find an answering lightness of being.

As you continue six times, a need to laugh.

25 We enter in to speak of sound.
Song, Souls of earth, has great effect
>   not only upon the physicality of your being but also,
>   upon the mentality of your being.

It effects even the cells within the brain.
Upon your earth you have machinery capable of various sounds.
Sounds that will destroy the eardrum, sounds that will split the heart.
You have instruments of music that soothe and comfort.
You have a great dichotomy between the two.
It is imperative that science understand the great comfort
>   that can be brought to humanity with the use of the gentle tones.

Do not misunderstand, Souls,
>   for all toning in gentleness is of comfort to mankind,
>   whether through the actual hearing of the tone by the ear
>   or by the body with the vibration,
>   as your great music master[9] composed much.

But the three instruments[10] hold greater power of sound vibration
>   to effect the being.

For those who wish to heal with the instruments of the earth,
>   then we would have you understand the tones that will effect
>   the various parts of the body using these three instruments.

The tones must be played gently, not raucous.

---

9 music master - in this case a reference to Beethoven

10 three instruments - drum, flute and violin. "Soul, we will say to you
the drum brings forth physical, mental healing.
The flute brings a connector to the high mind.
The violin is for the Soul who has melancholy, even depression.
It will admire the Soul's mind and seek to draw the Soul
from the depths and bring that mind to the heights of its purpose."

We would have you understand the tones, the level of the tones
> must be low, barely audible for the average.

It is only for the very young child under three
> that the tone may be just above audible.

The "A" tone for the top of the head from the eyebrow to the top.
All headaches, all injuries within that area,
> whether physical or mental emotional
> will be aided with the tone of "A".

The being is to sit in a quiet space.
It matters not if the being is deaf
> for they will respond to the vibration.

Lights are dimmed
> and the being sits thusly for fifteen minutes, thrice daily.

For those who are severely debilitated, you may increase to double.
The tone of "B" is for the area from the eyebrow to just above the heart.
The same procedure, the darkened room, the fifteen minutes.
The area from the heart to just below the bellybutton,
> is for the tone of "C".

It is for any ailments, disabilities, within that space of being.
The area from the bellybutton to the very base of the spine is for "D".
The same procedure, the darkened room, the fifteen minutes.
The area from the top of the thigh to below the knee
> is for the sound of "F".

The same procedure, the darkened room, the fifteen minutes.
From below the knee to the tip of the toes "G".
The same procedure, the darkened room, the fifteen minutes.
In cases of maladies that are minimal, results will be seen by the third day.
In more severe cases you will allow more time for results to appear.

Clarity

26 Each day, before you begin,
> place your forefingers and your thumbs together
> so that it forms a pyramidal shape.

Your other fingers are straight out, not touching.
Place this form upon that which you will work that day,
> whether it be paper, or canvas, or computer keyboard.

Hold the shape for fifteen seconds.
Place your head looking downward
> into the shape of the pyramid during the fifteen seconds.

At the end of the fifteen seconds, bring your hands upward,
    holding together the thumbs and the forefingers
in front of the third eye.
Hold for the count of seven.
Take a deep breath after the count of seven and whoosh it out.
Bring your hands downward,
    maintaining the position until they touch again
    the paper, the keyboard, the canvas.
Another deep breath.
Hold for another count of three.
Release your hands and begin your work.
This will assist in focusing the Energy of the eye,
    the Energy of Spirit upon that which you do.

27 We would have you understand the efficacy
    of movement of the hand and the arm upon a surface,
    whether it be sand, or paper or cloth.
The mere placing of your forefinger and then making a large S,
    and again another S, and then again a third S,
    is calming to one who has difficulty.
Repeating that motion will make great strides for clarity and focus.
Place other fingers closed, the thumb held loose as you draw.
The S need not be of any great width or length,
    simply your forefinger, until you have calmed your being.
It is the flow that will make the difference.
You will not get the same response
    from any other of your western alphabet,
    and it matters not what alphabet, what country,
    it is the flow of the S that makes the difference.
This would be most efficacious for any being;
    entering in to any exam for student, to an important meeting,
    to a practitioner who is as yet unsure of themselves,
    to the parents who are anxious over the child born or unborn.
It is also an efficacious prelude to a deeper meditation.
Many situations will benefit from this routine.

28 The holding of the hands upright,
    finger pad to finger pad, thumb pad to thumb pad
    in a prayer like position,

but not with the fingers closed or the palm closed;
this position, when held in front of the nasal and the mouth area,
is most efficacious for thought.
For those who must decipher, who must think through,
whether it be a problem or a study, it is most efficacious.
It focuses the mind.
The Energy from the palms forms a triad with the mind.

29 We would provide for you stretching exercises,
for the health and wellbeing of the mind.
To stretch the mind, use the syllable 'lah.'
It will not be advantageous to have it high or low, or even melodic,
it is simply the pronunciation of 'lah'.
Open your mouth wide as you pronounce it.
This exercise is to be done twelve times daily: lah lah lah.
You do not need to rush, do it at your own pace,
and understand it is the syllabication that is important.
The action of the tongue and the mouth opening wide,
and the sound all combine to exercise your mind,
to stimulate the mind.

30 Unto the gradation of color
where you begin to see more yellow than white,
know that this color is most efficacious
for those who hear voices that do not exist
except in their mind and require relief
from the constant barrage of noise,
for to them all sound becomes noise.
Placing this color around the eye and to the back of the head
and held in place for one half hour thrice daily
will bring about relief so that the being is able
to differentiate between normal sound and noise.
And the mind will begin to develop a clarity
as the mind absorbs the vibration of the color.

31 In any disagreement between beings,
especially between two like beings in a relationship,
whether it be friend or foe, or partner in a disagreement,
if one of the beings puts forth their hands, palm out,
even in the midst of great anger, of angry shouting,

a pause will occur and allow both parties to take a step back
and perhaps choose another alternative to settle their differences.

Depression
32 We would have you understand,
   there are many layers to what you call depression.
We would have you understand,
   there are many reasons for what you call depression.
It is an old Soul method of refusal to follow the path they have chosen.
It may also be a gift to another as a lesson, as a warning.
It may also be an opportunity to embrace and overcome a negativity.
Depression has both physical and emotionality.
A physical depression is often,
   and may be caused by toxins within the system
      affecting the brain matter,
      affecting the chemical composition of the brain itself,
      transferring to the mental state what you call a depression.
The body becomes unable to overcome the chemical changes
   brought about by the ingestion of toxins.
These toxins specifically are brought into the body
   through excessive amounts of alcohol.
And understand, Souls, that excessive amounts will vary
   depending upon the sensitivity of the Soul to alcohol,
   for each Soul has different sensitivity.
The chemical changes may also be brought about
   by the ingestion of smoke from the tobacco in all its forms.
It may also be brought about by those working within industries
   or shops or even in homes that work with tanning materials,
   dyeing materials, and industrial pollutants.
The odor from oils used in automobiles will cause a buildup over time
   that will alter the chemical composition and engender a depression.
Depression may also be brought about by the emotionality
   of those who reject calm, who need frenetic activity,
   who never or rarely rest the brain.
Again, this causes a chemical reaction,
   leading often to symptoms of depression.
It will alter the chemical composition of the brain
   and depending on sensitivity of the individual,
   it may cause a mild or severe episode.

33 We give unto you aroma.
The aroma of cloves is particularly enhancing for depression.
It is, Soul, not to be held directly underneath the nasal passages
    but off to the side, at least twenty four inches.
And burnt, if you wish,
    or simply place the oil of the clove upon a cloth
    and sit nearby for fifteen minutes.
The aroma will enter in and alter the mood.

34 Remedy for depression.
Roses and rosemary.
We would have you smell oil of roses.
We would have you waft the odor near the nostrils.
Not inhale deeply, but waft gently
    and recall with the scent of the roses, the summer sun,
    the warm gentle breezes, the green of the grass,
    and the leaves and the colors of roses; the reds,
    the oranges, the pinks, the white.
Waft the odor and place thy being within the realm of healing colors,
    sights and sounds.
We ask that you place within food
    one eighth teaspoon of rosemary daily,
    not cooked, placed on top of the food.
If the Soul is not in acceptance, it is not the solution.

35 For those who are in a depression of spirit,
    give unto them a bouquet of phlox and it will lift the spirit.
Have them gaze upon the phlox and hold the phlox bouquet
    encompassed in their hands for only a moment
    and it will lift the spirit.

36 For those who are in depressive mode,
    we recommend the addition of one drop of geranium oil
    to one quarter cup olive oil.
It will be massaged into the feet
    and also correspondingly massaged into the hands.

37 When feeling depressed, three times wash the hands
    with the pure peppermint tea and inhale the aroma.

This will wake up the centers of the mind and release endorphins.
If you are using fresh pure peppermint leaves
> you need only four large leaves to be boiled for three minutes
> within one and a half cups water.

38 Souls of earth, we would have you understand,
> the gradations of color have an effect upon the psyche of a being.

No color utilized for healing, whether in the full complete shade
> or whether in a slight gradation of the full shade, can harm a being.

This we would have you understand.
Having understood this, you will also understand
> that gradations of color affect the psyche
> and the physicality in a different manner.

We will give unto you other gradations of depression
> and other gradations of color that will affect the depression.

For those Souls who have awareness
> of when they are entering in to a depression,
> in the first throes of this dread disease,
> a gentle mauve with a hint of violet placed about the being,
> gazed upon will give the impetus to stop entering any further
> into the depression and help the Soul rise out.

A Soul who has entered in to a depression, but of a mild nature,
> who has yet to be aware of the depression, will benefit from violet.

And the being who has been in a deeper mode of depression,
> but not yet severe, will benefit
> from the shade between violet and purple.

It would behoove the beings to use this daily
> and throughout the day for a period of three days.

And they will then notice the difference and become aware of the difference
> as they begin to rise out of the depths.

Even, Souls of earth, for those who have a affinity for the stone,
> a small amethyst held within the palm will be of great benefit.

The amethyst must follow the shades we have given.
For as you know, it comes in many shades and gradations of color.
It is not enough to wear it about your being
> when it is being used for a depressive state.

When used for assistance in the depressive state
> it must be held within the palm.

Held within both palms is even more effective.

And, if using this methodology, you are to hold it within the palms
    for at least three minutes each time and often throughout your day.

39 Souls of earth, we would speak of the color purple.
We would have you understand all beings, human, upon your earth plane,
    have a built in affinity for the color purple.
It is often superimposed by the mood of the being
    and therefore, submerged and not allowed to surface.
And so, we are using the color purple as an additive to healing.
You will understand that some beings will totally reject,
    and that is because, at that point in time,
    their overwhelming depressive state.
All depressives will mute or totally ignore the color of purple.
It is because in their psyche it is much too bright and so instinctively,
    in the depressive state, push it from their beings,
    unknowing that it will assist in rising out of the depression.
Understand, those of you who are in a severe depressive state,
    wrap yourself in purple.
Even though, your psyche and even though your being is repelled,
    wrap your being in purple.
It can be a cloth, it can be in your mind
    enveloping yourself in a cloud of purple.
It can be in a painting that you gaze upon.
But understand, it will break, it will fracture the drear of being
    and allow you to begin to rise out of that depression.
We offer this unto you as one of many solutions, but as one
    that of a certainty will be of assistance to the psyche of your being.

40 In the gradation of green, what you would call, a mint green,
    this is for those Souls who are entering in to a mild depression.
It will alleviate the depression and in many cases stop before it begins fully.
This color is to be worn as a shirt would be worn
    and it is to be worn throughout the day and throughout the night
    until the episode is no longer apparent.
This mint green color is also efficacious
    to be placed within rooms of those prone to depression,
    prone to hopelessness brought about by illness or emotional distress.

Even worn as a ribbon on the wrist, it will help, Souls of earth,
    for it carries a very open healing vibration.

41 Madonna blue color is also for those
    who have fallen deep into depression,
    for those who have fallen deep into grief,
    who feel that their heart is breaking
    and they can no longer tolerate the pain.

42 Further shading into a darker blue, not yet into the dark blue,
    only a shade beyond medium blue,
    this is for those Souls entering in to depression.
Not the Soul already in a depression but those entering to,
    those teetering on the verge
    and those who have entered in to grieving,
    it will assist.
The families of those who are leaving will benefit from this color,
    it will assist in their coping.

43 Into the very end of the spectrum, into the very deepest of yellow,
    gaze upon this color, those who are in sore despair,
    desperate in any case whether it be physical or mental.
For the deepest of depressions, gaze upon this color,
    immerse thy being in this color and know wellness.
Wear upon thy wrist this color, in a band at least an inch in width,
    daily, until the episode has passed.
Place about thy being, in the area of the neck, this color
      and hold it close to the throat area for fifteen minutes, thrice daily
      and know healing.
It will assist, to bring out of a severe depression, a being.
It will give hope to that being.
It will give a taste for life to that being.
The deepest yellow is for anyone who has lost the joy of life,
    and needs the spur to regain their balance.

44 We would speak on the properties on the color of coral.
The coral that has a reddish hue, not the pink.

Coral is a color that is most efficacious
> when worn by beings who have an attitude of futility,
> of hopelessness you would call it,
> these beings caught in the grip of this powerful emotion.

When wearing the color of coral, they will find it easier
> to overcome, to reach unto the hope, to reach
> unto possibilities of solutions.

The coral may be worn as a garment,
> or it may be worn as ribbons around the wrist area,
> around the ankle area.

The vibration of the color will enter in to the being.

The ribbon need not be wide,
> an inch is sufficient whether at the ankles or the wrist.

It may also be used as a ribbon around the neck.

Gazing upon a picture of the color of coral will assist
> in bringing one out of the depths.

Placing bits of coral color about the room of an ill being
> that has lost hope will ameliorate that despair.

A blanket, a covering, a sheet in that color
> will help the most intense despair of futility.

Those beings who feel they are in the last stages of illness
> would find it most efficacious to have a covering of this coral color.

For the babe whose mother is in despair,
> if the mother chooses not to use the color
> we would suggest you place it upon the child,
> for the child is affected by your hopeless and futility,
> and it will help the child to regain its own balance.

Coral in this shade provides a lift to the psyche.

Even, Soul, if the being is blind with earth eyes it may be seen with the eye
> and it is the vibration of the color that is felt by the body.

Indeed it is felt by the skin of the body when placed upon the skin.

And the skin alerts the cells and the psyche that all is not futile.

45 Beings who are in a state of depression,
> will find it most efficacious to stride as long a stride as possible,
> within a ten minute period.

The striding invigorates the body
> but also enervates the cells involved in the depression.

Ten minutes daily of striding is most efficacious
> for overcoming depression.

Autism

46 We would address autism.
Many of the beings labeled with the term autism have been misdiagnosed.
Those who have been misdiagnosed are more than likely beings
    who have such overwhelming fears of earth,
    that they enter in to themselves and refuse to come out.
Careful caring of these Souls and drawing out those things that they fear,
    and helping them to overcome them,
    will bring about a marked change in these beings.
Prevalent fears include loud voices, and to them,
    afflicted with this fear, loud would be to your ears a normal tone.
Speaking only in a gentle almost whisper to these beings
    will gain their attention; for the loud voice,
    which we term as normal, will only cause them to retreat.
The other common prevalent fear is that of light.
All incandescent light causes a buzzing within their minds
    and irritation that they retreat from
    and try through various methodologies to ignore.
The repetitive motion of beings of the afflicted ones is oft times just that.
To try to get away from the constant buzzing in their mind.
Take this into account in the rooms where these beings live and play.
The other prevalent common fears of these beings
    will be reflected from the people around them.
For they fear anger.
It only needs to be in a being and they retreat from it.
The hitting of self is fear of that anger being turned upon them.
And so they punish self first in the hopes of keeping the anger away.
All beings caring for these afflicted ones
    must enter in to their space in loving calmness,
    to alleviate this fear, to help them overcome this fear.
Play is one of the most healing modalities for these afflicted ones.
Play, laughter, even raucous laughter,
    it need not be gentle laughter, will penetrate the barriers.
Gentle, soft, back ground music, that gentle music of Brahms
    and some of the gentle music of Mozart
    is conducive to calm for their beings.
The laughter attracts their attention.
The play must be unstructured.
The play, done in loving calmness,
    must appeal to the overcoming of their fears.

And so in the play you would avoid those common fears
    so as not to stress the being.
Color is an addition that will have positive effect upon the afflicted ones.
The colors must all be soft gradations of color,
    colors in the beginning stages of each spectrum of orange,
    of yellow, of green, of blue, and violet.
And so wherever they work, play, live,
    only the softest of colors should be present.
Not just within the walls that are painted,
    but within the coverings of windows,
    within the coverings of the bed,
    within even the coverings of the table upon which they play or eat.
The furniture is also covered with these soft colors.
The object is to create the feeling
    of soothing, loving, comfort, and calm, so that it enables
    the being to enter out from their self imposed barriers,
    to enter out safely in a secure environment.
We would also suggest that foods play a part
    in the recovery of the autistic being.
We would suggest no meats,
    for the chemicals within the meats
    react negatively upon the brainwaves.
All manner of vegetables may be served.
All colors of potatoes and squash may be served.
We would suggest dairy products be kept to a minimum
    and served only thrice weekly,
    and no more than four ounces per serving.
We would have the beings refrain from all wheat products
    until they have improved and then wheat may be served
    once a week.
We would also encourage no food dyes,
    not red, not blue, not yellow, none.
The only food dye that is permissible
    is that which is naturally found in the blueberries.
Read carefully the labels of the food stuffs
    so that no artificial sugars are present.
The Souls may have sugar in the form of honey.
Refrain from fizz drinks,
    for the carbonation is inimical to these beings.
Caffeine is also inimical to these beings.

Caffeine in any form, whether in fizz or in coffee or in tea,
> sets up within the brain a buzzing
> and distorts the metabolism of these beings.

Rice may be used once a week
> and we would suggest the brown rice.

All manner of nuts are acceptable.
We would caution those nuts that are soaked
> in cottonseed oil or palm oil are to be ingested,
> only once per week, three ounces.

All others are acceptable.
Use only olive oil for cooking or baking for these beings.

47 The child who is autistic, even unto catatonic,
> will benefit from this color, from this shade,
> a shade further into a darker blue from the eggshell blue.

Understand it is placed with compassion,
> not simply to quiet the being but to give forth compassion.

Alzheimer

48 The macadamia nut oil[11] mixed with geranium oil
> is most efficacious also for the Alzheimer patient
> who is possessed of much anger and fear.

In this case it may be done three times per day.
It is one half teaspoon of the oil, one drop geranium
> and then lightly placed with the forefinger,
> across the middle of the brow
> approximately one half hour before sleep time.

The being will be soothed.

49 The stronger the shade of pink,
> the more vibration will enter in to the being.

The very aged who are affected with various diseases
> such as the Alzheimer,
> will benefit from this shade of strong pink being given to them.

It would be best to place within their room, this color.
Even a small scrap of cloth, that they may hold to them,
> will ease the jitteriness, the crankiness.

---

11 Caution: use only oil from Macadamia integrifolia and Macadamia tetraphylla.

50 For those who have access to the kelp beds,
   especially that dark, dark green,
   we would draw your attention to the bulb.
For within the bulb are healing properties.
Open the bulb, and dip your finger in.
Place small amount, dab lightly,
   starting from the brow line down the nostril
   and under the eye and then out to the tip of the ears.
This will assist those beings who have Alzheimer,
   who are in agitation of the mind.
This may be done as often as necessary, to calm the being.

Stress
51 We would have humanity understand
   the very detrimental and deleterious effects of stress
   upon the blood pressure.
For it is the mind that engages in, that encapsulates stress
   and it is the body and the heart that must deal then
   with the effects caused by the stress.
To begin to break the pattern of daily living in stress,
   we would have you begin with one quarter teaspoon olive oil
      mixed with one quarter teaspoon baking soda.
This is to be ingested daily for a period of seven days.
And then, Souls of earth, refrain from this for a period of three days.
And then for a period of seven days,
   one quarter teaspoon olive oil and cream of tartar.
At the end of the seven days, rest three days.
And then daily place upon either wrist
   one drop lavender oil and smooth it in.
Each day this is to be done until the body recognizes
   it no longer has to cope with the stress of the mind.
The mind will have the opportunity to cease its pattern of destruction.
And we would ask during these period of days,
   that as soon as you observe your being stressing,
   that you place the thumb and the forefinger together on each hand.
And then bring the two together tapping each other, taking a deep breath
   and as soon as the stress begins to leave, cease.
And your body and your mind are being re patterned.

52 The steam from the jasmine is most efficacious
for those being who find themselves anxious,
whether for known cause or unknown cause;
it will soothe the mentality.
Place two drops jasmine oil in a quart of boiling water.

53 To those who are experiencing panic attacks, anxiety, stress,
who worry their beings,
an application to the sole of each foot
and to the glands on the outer area of the throat:
one quarter cup olive oil, one drop lavender, one drop geranium.
This will assist in calming the being.
These remedies may be used at any age from newborn to the very elderly.

54 The macadamia nut oil[12] mixed with geranium oil
is most efficacious for the troubled Soul who has night terrors.
It is one half teaspoon of the oil, one drop geranium
and then lightly placed with the forefinger,
across the middle of the brow
approximately one half hour before sleep time.
The being will be soothed.

55 We particularly draw your attention to the verbena
that is the color purple for it has the most power
to assist in overcoming the deleterious effects of stress
upon the body and the mind.
You do not have to make concoctions.
You are merely gathering grains as a honey bee might gather nectar.
It is not the leaves or the root but the very center at the top.
Grasp with thy fingers, not with the sharpness of knife or scissors.
Place it gently under the tongue.
Only a minute amount is necessary.
Ten grains will within three days, done daily,
bring a balance to a troubled being.
And it will bring surcease to the ravages of stress upon the body.
Do you see, Souls of earth, how wondrous is our Creator who gives to us
all manner of remedies for our ills, whether they be of mind or body.

---

12 Caution: use only oil from Macadamia integrifolia and Macadamia tetraphylla.

Sleep

56 Sleeping problem.
We would have you understand the effect of worry
    upon the body and the mind.
It depletes all your reserves.
It coalesces negativity into the predominant state of being
    thereby ensuring the body stressors to intimidate the mind.
We would suggest the following physical remedy;
    no stimuli after five o'clock p.m..
For two weeks, no caffeine, no spices.
At six o'clock p.m. one cup of chamomile tea, steeped for five minutes
    with the addition of a dollop of honey and some milk.
Drink slowly.
At seven o'clock p.m. one more cup of chamomile with the honey and milk.
Then place one drop geranium each week at the head of the mattress,
    not on the pillow.
During the day, rest for twenty minutes twice daily.
Within two weeks this regime will bring about
    a change in your sleeping patterns.

57 We would have you understand the oil of the garlic
    has a calming effect, when gently taking the split clove of garlic
    and rubbing it lightly upon the soles of the feet
    and upon the palms of the hand.
It is most efficacious for those beings who have difficulty sleeping
    because of the tension, the stress, the franticness of the mind.
A dab on the palms and on the sole of the foot beneath the large toe.

58 We give unto you an exercise for insomniacs
    for those beings who pace, who toss and turn,
        who give up trying to sleep, who worry about sleep.
Complete this exercise three times in the half hour
    before you enter in to sleep mode.
This will assist you to break the cycle of insomnia.
This will relax your inner being to allow the sleep to take place.
Step 1
One half hour before you would normally enter in to your sleep mode,
    you will take the thumbs and forefingers and make a circle;
        right to right, left to left, the other fingers held loosely.

Step 2
Bring the thumb and forefinger circles up
   so that they are actually touching the closed eyes.

Step 3
Fold down the other fingers,
   and hold them close into the palm of the hand.

Step 4
Maintain one of the hands with the fingers folded down and
   the thumb and forefinger making a circle until Step 10.

Step 4
Take one of the circled thumbs and forefingers, open
   and press lightly unto the bridge of the nose on either side
   and pinch slowly the flesh; not to harm, simply to pressure.

Step 5
As you are doing that, Soul,
   you will take and make the following with your lips five times:
   phew phew phew phew phew.
You will feel, if you are doing it correctly, in your solar plexus.
You will feel it just below the rib cage.

Step 6
Take a deep breath and exhale.

Step 7
Repeat Steps 4 and 5.

Step 8
Take another deep breath and exhale.

Step 9
And once more repeat Steps 4 and 5.
Stop, take a breath and then five more times.

Step 10
And then, Souls, open up the fingers,
    open up the thumb and forefinger.

59 We would have a suggestion, Souls of earth,
    and that is that you daily hug your being before retiring.
A restful sleep without stress, without worry,
    without strain is imperative for a balanced being.
It is not so much, Soul, the length of time that you spend asleep,
    it is the quality of time you spend asleep
    that is important for balanced well being.
The hug begins with the right hand upon the left breast,
    and the left hand upon the right breast.
You will note your wrists are crossed if you have the right position.
And then simply press the hands gently inward
    and move the shoulders forward slightly,
    hold for three seconds and then relax,
    move your left away, move your right away;
    and you will note as you do so, a tingling,
    a pressure upon the forehead.
And you will understand that you will have a more relaxed quality of sleep.

Instability
60 We would speak of mental instability.
We would have you understand to get to the basis,
    to the root of a mental instability,
    it is necessary to delve into the tastes,
    the gravitation of foods to that being and know
    that that particular food and in rare cases combination of foods
    has caused a reaction within the chemical balance within the body.
What you call episodic events
    in those who have a diagnose as mentally unstable,
    is merely an overindulgence
    in that particular food that they are drawn to.
It takes some study time to ascertain which food
    contributes to the instability
    and then it is the gradual reduction and the eventual abstention
    of that food that will bring about balance.

61 For those who are in the midst of schizophrenia,
     the color must go to a deeper shade of blue,
     only a shade further into a darker blue from the eggshell blue.
Place the cloth, enwrap the being in the color.
Their Soul will enter in to that vibration and it will bring
     a momentary balancing, a stabilization for the being.

Head

Scalp

62 For seborrhea, psoriasis, dry scalp,
    redness and itching of the scalp,
    we would speak of the rose that has efficacious properties.
Place within the hand twelve rose petals,
    preferably in the red to pink color, for the Energy is stronger.
Place between the palms and hold for thirty two seconds
    to give them a slight warmth in temperature
    and also to imbue them with Energy, your sacred Energy.
Then take the petals and place them within a bowl of water,
    room temperature, enough water to cover the petals.
Gently tap down each petal at least once.
And then let them rise if they wish.
They will stay within the bowl of water for one full day,
    twenty four hours.
These rose petals are to have no pesticides placed upon them,
    no chemicals placed upon them.
The actual plant is to have no pesticides added to the ground
    where upon it grows, no chemicals.
There will be, of course, since toxins float in your air,
    a certain amount of toxicity, but we would not have you add to it.
Preferably we find most efficacious that which you call wild roses.
Those that were placed here in their original state
    and before they became hybrid.
For the wild roses contain the most Energy and are the most efficacious.
Indeed, the hybrids still retain some of the original but in a diluted form.
After the twenty four hours,
    the rose petals may be separated from the water,

the water to be placed in a glass container with a cork or cloth top,
so that there is an allowance of some air to enter in.
Within one cup of water of the roses, place one drop of honey,
one drop of rosemary, one drop pure peppermint
and one quarter teaspoon cinnamon.
Mixed and placed upon the scalp it will alleviate
what you call seborrhea, psoriasis, dry scalp,
redness and itching of the scalp.
Allow the remedy to stay in the scalp for one half hour
and then it may be washed.

63 When the scalp has been attacked by sebaceous cysts,
by dermatitis, dandruff, by any itching of the scalp,
place one half teaspoon garlic oil into one tablespoon olive oil.
Massage it into the scalp and let sit for six minutes and then wash.
You will find almost instant relief in most cases.

64 The frangipani flower is most efficacious when dried,
for in drying it becomes concentrated.
The fresh does not have as much efficacy,
in this particular case as the dried.
Once it is dried, grind it into a fine powder.
This powder, a very minute amount, may be then mixed with water
and placed upon the scalp of those who have eczema,
of those who have psoriasis of the scalp,
of those who have any scalp eruptions.
Simply smooth it on to the scalp.
You may also use olive oil should a pure water not be available.
This powder when placed within a glass container
and stored with a cloth over, natural cloth, in a dark place,
will last for years before it loses its potency.

65 Scrape the outer edge of the pine bark.
The piece will be no more than three inches by three inches.
This may be ground into a fine, fine powder.
Make from this a tea.
The tea may be used as a rinse for the scalp full of sores,
or in that you call cradle cap.

Dilute three cups water to one cup tea
>and use as a rinse upon the head,
>after cleansing the scalp.
It will help to soothe the sores.

Headache

66 Deeper into the color of green so that is beyond the pales
>and yet not full into the spectrum of green,
>this color needs to be worn by those
>who have the headache from tension,
>specifically tension causing headaches.

It may be most efficacious when placed upon the forehead.
It may also be worn about the neck.

67 The root of the star anise may be ground finely into a powder
>and the powder will relieve all headaches and all anxieties.

It has a calming effect upon the veins that would constrict
>in the case of a headache
>and those that constrict in the case of anxiety.

A minute amount of powder is all that is necessary
>to relieve pain and discomfort.

To be a remedy, the powder needs only the finger
>dipped lightly and placed upon the tongue.

68 We would speak on the properties of salal.
We would have you understand
>for those who have headache, this is a handy remedy.

Take a minimum of six leaves,
>smooth upon each leaf, olive oil
>only to help the leaves to stay upon the head.

Place upon each eye, and across the forehead.
>for fifteen minutes
>for those who have medium to severe pain.

For those who have lighter headaches,
>only until the headache eases.

Holding your head back or in a prone position,
>for a period of four seconds place slight pressure
>upon the ears inside, almost as if you were cutting out sound.

After you remove the salal from the eyes and the forehead,
    then take two fingers and rub gently the temples
    to remove any dregs of pain left.
Rub them in a circular motion together at the same time.

69 For those who have the sinus headache,
    any headache caused by injury to the face,
    or bones of the face, injury caused by the skull,
    you may take a handful of juniper leaves,
    place in boiling water.
For three cups of water,
    no more than one quarter cup is necessary.
Stir for one minute,
    let sit for three minutes, strain
    and you will have a tea.
The juniper leaves that were in the boiling water
    and that you have strained out, may be retained for a poultice.
Placed within muslin or a cheesecloth warmed
    and allow to sit upon the brow for fifteen minutes.

70 We would speak on the properties of fireweed.
You have, Souls of earth, a plant that grows wild and may be cultivated.
We would have you understand the stamen of the fireweed
    is particularly efficacious when made powdery,
    ground simply with your fingers,
    and then, gently inhaled,
This will clear the sinuses, will relieve any sinus complications
    such as headaches or stuffiness,
    or pain within the outer areas such as underneath the eyes.
You need only the powder from one.
It is not necessary to ingest volumes.
This may be done three times daily.

71 Soul, migraines are in the majority of cases,
    caused by a physical constriction of the blood vessels.
Not in the brain, but at the base of the neck
    which prevents full flowing to the brain.
Hence the pain.

There are, Soul, a variety of causes for migraines in all their forms.
We would suggest when you arise in the mornings
    or at anytime when you have been in a prone position,
    that you turn onto your right side slowly,
    and slowly lift the upper torso into a sitting position
    on the side of the bed or the couch.
Do not jump up or quickly lift up the head.
We would also suggest that when in the throes of migraine
    that you ensure there is no pressure on the back of the neck.
When you are in a prone position,
    do not lay on your back when in the throes of migraine.
You will also, in the throes of migraine,
    place warm cloth on the back of the neck,
    not cold, warm and apply for ten minutes.
When the cloth is cool, warm it and it should be moist.
We would also suggest
    to not only alleviate but to also prevent further recurrences,
    a daily, feathery, light massage.
You will then place on either side of the back of the neck
    where you will sense and feel a throbbing,
    and then you will do the tickling on the back of the neck,
    but gently.
Start at outer edge and enter inward,
    and hold gentle pressure for a count of ten.

72 Indeed migraines are common upon the earth.
And there has always been a variety of causes for the migraines.
We would suggest that at the first inkling, the eyes are shut,
    a dark mask is placed over the eyes
    and a very gentle rotation clockwise of both temples,
    and then gradually moving back unto the middle of the ear
    and then pressing with the two fingers on both sides
    for a period of five seconds and then do not release quickly,
    release slowly.
And again, thrice and allow the pain to leave.
We would suggest that you cease any and all types of dairy,
    all, no exception at any time during a migraine.
And within, Soul, a matter of weeks you will notice
    a lessening of the severity and the number of incidences.

73 Before the full onslaught of the migraine,
    we would ask that the bottom of the feet are gently massaged
    with a combination of one quarter cup olive oil,
    one drop jasmine, one drop lavender
    and one drop of geranium oil on the whole sole.
A gentle placement of the mixture in a circular motion, clockwise,
    starting underneath the toes
    and going down the full length of the feet,
    ending just below the ankle,
    once on either foot.
The rubbing, the massaging of the concoction into the soles of the feet
    will assist in the relaxation, allow the meridians,
    allowing the vessels to stay open.
After the soles of the feet are massaged,
    across the neck where the jugular is,
    place a dab of the concoction,
    and also the back of the neck.
And you will experience a receding, an ebbing of those symptoms
    that are the precursor to the full blown migraine.

74 Acupressure points for those who have a difficulty
    of constricting veins for the migraines.
Using the forefinger and the finger next to it
    place, not directly on the spine,
    but at either side of the spine at the back of the neck,
    midway between the very base of the head
    and the beginning of the shoulder area,
    and apply pressure.
The pressure is to be light but firm
    for five seconds.
Then place the fingers in a line of an arc above the ears
    and press gently all the fingertips.
And then take your thumbs
    and place on either side of the throat
    and press gently but firmly.
And you are to hold this until the pulsation begins,
    but for no more than fifteen seconds each time.
If pulsation has not began at the end of the fifteen seconds,
    remove your fingers and hands for a period of fifteen minutes

and then proceed again until you have relieved
and indeed deleted your headache, your migraine.

75 The properties of the Mulberry Bush.
Study the leaves and you will notice
    some are a shade lighter than others.
We would have you disregard the lighter shaded leaves.
They are not to be used in any potion or mixture.
You will liken unto only the deep shaded, shining leaves.
You will notice the leaves have points
    and it is the points that contain the efficacious properties
    to relieve the serious migraine.
The leaves may be plucked from the plant, ten leaves.
Then remove only the outer edge of the leaf, eight centimeters.
Then slice the outer edges into minute portions and brew.
Once the purified water in which these are brewed has become discolored,
    they are then ready to be placed directly upon the temples.
They are to be placed on both sides in equal measure.
You will place cloth about the skull to hold them in place.
This is to be done each hour until the symptoms have receded.
The room will remain dark, the eyes remain closed.
And Souls, we would caution those who are prone to migraine
    to restrict the intake of sugars.
It will not totally prevent but it will mitigate and minimize any occurrence.

76 Honey is soothing to the sufferers of migraine.
Mix one quarter teaspoon of the honey to one tablespoon of olive oil.
Place lightly upon the eyelids
    and from the middle of the forehead unto the temples.
Keeping the eyes closed and laying down in a prone position
    for at least twenty five minutes,
    you will feel a lessening of the intensity of the pain.

Eyes
77 We would discuss with you pressure points.
Thumbs and forefingers together,
    other fingers touching at the fingertips.
For sore, aching, red, swollen eyes,
    place in front of the eyes the circles

made by the thumb and forefingers together,
    thumbs and forefingers will be touching each other.
Hold that position and move your thumb and forefingers up and down,
    up and down in front of your eyes.
Do this eleven times, pause,
    deep breath, and do it two more times.
And you will feel a great relief on the eyes.

78 Pressure points for the blurred vision,
The thumbs and forefingers held together,
    and entwine your fingers,
Bring them up in front of your eyes.
Move your thumb and forefinger
    back and forth seven times.
Pause and take a breath.
Move your fingers apart,
    and then back again seven more times.
And then remove the thumbs and forefingers first,
    and then your fingers.
This will also assist in calming the effects of macular degeneration[13].

79 To slow down macular degeneration, make
    a paste of carrot and spinach[14],
    boiled until they become soft,
    mashed until the juices start to flow.
The juice is then removed and placed upon the eyelid.
It is not necessary to place on the eye itself.
The eyelid will absorb the healing properties of this remedy.
And it will slow.

80 For those who have the cataract,
    we would recommend the bathing of the eye.
Again, Souls of earth, not the inner eye,
    not the corner of the eye, but the eyelids with
    a mixture of one half teaspoon of sea salt,

---

13 *Will that affect both kinds of macular degeneration?*
It is for the dry, Soul.

14 carrot and spinach – one half cup carrots, one half cup spinach.

one half teaspoon brown kelp,
  in one quarter cup olive oil, mixed thoroughly.
The kelp may be placed as is or it may be dried form.
This concoction will then be placed upon the eyelids,
  underneath the eyes and in the center of the forehead.
Again, the position must be the eyes looking up, with the eyelids closed.
This is to be done to both eyes, even if the cataract is only on one eye.
And this is only most efficacious with the beginning of a cataract.
This is to be done, four times per day,
    for a period of three weeks,
    and then twice per day until the condition has improved.

81 The inside banana peel is helpful
    for those beings who have allergies that attack the eyes.
You would, Soul, merely close the eyes,
    gently rub the lid of each eye
    and then place over both eyes the peel.
Allow it to lay against the eyes until the allergy eases.

82 We would speak on the properties of salal.
We would have you understand, the leaves of the salal,
    especially in their young state, freshly budded,
    are efficacious for the eyes.
Any irritation of the eye caused by wind or air
    will be assisted by this method.
For those who have allergies where the eyes are affected,
    this is most efficacious.
Before placing upon the eyelids
    smooth upon each leaf olive oil,
    to hold the leaves in place
    and assist them in the releasing of their healing properties.
Place three leaves upon each eyelid
    for a period of one minute.

83 For those who experience the itchy watery eyes
    and can find no apparent reason for such an affliction,
    we would recommend the placement upon the eyelids
    of cucumber, a slice upon each eyelid,
    or squash, particularly the zucchini squash,

a slice placed upon each eyelid
and left for a period of one minute.
And then you may find your eyes are soothed.

84 We would direct your attention to the milkweed[15].
It is a plant that may assist in the healing of ocularity.
Within the moisture the drops that you refer to as milk
    within this plant called milkweed, are efficacious applications.
It is as the droplet begins to form that you take a dropper
    cleansed before in the salt water and the boiling water.
Then you may take the dropper and touch upon a glass plate
    the droplets as they form upon the head of the plant.
As you gather droplets you will then ingest them into the dropper
    and into a cleansed glass vial, a container.
Souls of earth, you do not require massive amounts of this plant
    for healing purposes.
The properties of the plant are potent.
Once you have the droplets within the vial, they too must be purified.
One droplet placed in corner at ends of the affected eye, not in the eye,
    will remedy any irritation forming within the eye,
    an irritation that you refer to as an infection.
It is to be placed such, three times daily until remission of infection.

85 For eyes who can not see far distance,
    we would suggest the placement of oil of bergamot
    mixed one drop to one tablespoon of olive oil
    upon the outer lids of the eye and beneath the eye.
Not, Souls of earth, upon the corners and not upon the eye itself.
It is enough that it is upon the lids for the lids will filter for the eyes.
The placement of this oil is to be in the very lightest of film, not thickly.
It is to be done five times per day upon both eyes.
Whether laying down or sitting up, the head is to be so
    that the eyes are looking straight up, not forward,
    with the eyelids closed for thirty one seconds.

86 For those who have difficulty seeing short distances, close up,
    we would suggest the oil of cinnamon.

---

15 CAUTION: use only non-toxic species of milkweed.

Dilute one drop of oil of cinnamon to two tablespoons of olive oil.
This is placed upon the eyelids
    and underneath the eye in a light film for thirty two seconds
    three times per day until the condition improves.
It is not to be placed on the corners of the eye or in the eye.
The head is placed in a position so that the eyes
    are looking straight up with the eyelids closed.

Ears
87 A build up in your ear which presses upon the drum.
We would suggest that you apply
    a warm drop of olive oil mixed with a drop of lavender.
Warm, not hot, Soul.
Tilt the head and place within a cotton
    to hold the drops until they absorb.
This may be done three times daily to loosen the buildup.

88 The flower of the phlox, five petals,
    ground once they are dried, into a fine powder
    is efficacious when used with the earache.
You will place a dab of olive oil upon a digit, dip it into the powder,
    and place that at the outer edge of the inner canal,
    gently massaging it in.
This may be done once every hour until the pain is alleviated,
    whether it is for the baby or the adult.

89 The bud of the strawberry before it ripens,
    before it begins to turn color,
    may be used as a tea for the earaches.
For one cup of tea, six of the green berries steeped in hot water,
    allowed to sit within the hot water for five minutes.
Strain the berries and then apply the tea to the back of the ear
    both fully covering the ear and the skull next to the ear.
Allow to dry upon the skin.
Pay particular attention that it is in the crease
    between the ear and the skull.
Ensure that that is wet with the tea.
Place it also upon the frontal edge of the ear.

90 For earaches, the oat grass is to be cut
   when it reaches the height of only two inches.
You will place no more than twenty pieces of the grass
   within no more than one quarter cup of warm water.
Leave the grass and the water covered for a period of five days.
At the end of the five days the water may be bottled
   and placed within container for later use.
This concoction, after you strain from it the grass,
   is efficacious for earaches.
Use a cloth to swab gently the ears of either child or adult.
It may also be used for the feline or canine.

91 Unto the gradation of color
   where you begin to see more yellow than white.
When you see more yellow than white,
   know that this color is most efficacious
   for those who have the ringing in the ear,
   to the point where they are desperate for relief.
It will be placed upon both ears and left there
   for fifteen minutes, thrice daily until the ringing stops.

Nose

92 For the being who has a broken nose,
   a broken mouth area, a broken jaw area,
   the deep purple pansies will be most efficacious.
Take five of the whole flowers, grind them until they separate.
Once they have separated, place one tablespoon of water in the bowl
   along with one eighth teaspoon of salt.
It may be sea salt or ground salt.
Let that sit for a period of forty five minutes.
Then grind again until you have a paste.
Place that paste directly upon the broken area,
   wherever it is on the face.
Hold it, pressing very lightly the broken area
   for a minimum of twelve minutes.
You may place bandage to hold it in place
   or you may simply hold it in your hand.
This will reduce the swelling
   and stimulate the healing of the broken area.

93 For the stuffed nose that inhibits the restful sleep,
   with the right hand,
      place the thumb against all four fingers.
Place upon the forehead the four fingers
      and ensure that the cupped palm
      is facing the bridge of the nose
      and your fingers and thumb are resting upon the forehead.
Your other hand, place the fingers close together,
      your thumb and forefinger touching,
      and press inward lightly, once, twice, thrice
         underneath the nose, between the lip and the bottom of the nose,
And you will be able to enter in to a more restful sleep.

94   The juniper, no matter the variety, is efficacious.
Six leaves when pulled gently, whether it be a tree or a bush,
      and rubbed gently between the thumb and the first two fingers,
      give forth an aroma.
The aroma is helpful to those who have allergies and sinus congestion.
As you breathe it in, it soothes the irritated passages of the nose
      and it soothes the irritation of the eyes from allergies.
It interacts with the oils within your skin and assists in ameliorating.

95   A tea of catnip is efficacious for those who are prone to allergies.
One half teaspoon to a cup of water,
      steep the same as your black tea, as your herbal tea,
      but you would not, Soul, steep it more than one minute.

Mouth
96   We would have you understand the very properties
         of what you call your wallflower have efficacious benefits.
Five petals, placed between the thumb and the forefinger,
      and mushed until they become one moist petal,
         placed underneath the tongue for seven seconds is most efficacious
         for thrush of the mouth.
For the more severe cases this is done every three hours
      until a subsiding of the thrush and then
      once every four hours until it has totally subsided.
It is the same whether it attacks an infant or adult.

The child, nor the adult, will swallow;
> they will remove the glob after it has been underneath the tongue for seven seconds.

The beings will also take another five petals, again mold them together
> until they become moist and they become one,
> and then rub the moisture along the bottom
> between the bottom of the lip and the chin;
> back and forth until it shreds.

This will, Soul, have a two approach, inside and out, to the thrush.

97 Leaf of pure peppermint
> is efficacious for those who have Candida,
> for those who have thrush of the mouth.

For those who have the Candida,
> three leaves held underneath the tongue
> for a period of thirty two seconds,
> so that the system absorbs the efficacy of the leaves.

For those who have the thrush of the mouth
> they will require five leaves.

The leaves are minuscule.
They do not need to be huge.
The small leaf is best as it first buds from the plant.
As soon as it is opened, Soul, it is in its peak of efficacy.

98 For thrush, the outer bark of the holly tree,
> a small one by one inch square placed within one fourth cup water,
> and allowed to sit for three days
> and then the water may be swished in the mouth for thrush.

It will not harm the being if some water is swallowed.

99 We would speak today on the properties
> of the pure peppermint plant.

It is true that there are many varieties within the pure mint family
> and pure mint has its place as an efficacious healing adjunct.

But it is the pure peppermint that is most efficacious
> in cases of mouth sores, of gum disease,
> of tongue eruptions, of thrush,
> of those open ulcers oft times found within the mouth area.

The oil of pure peppermint is highly concentrated
    and therefore will not be used when there is an open sore.
For open sores within the mouth area,
    we would suggest the pure peppermint tea.
Using leaves,
    use one tablespoon to one half cup water
    steeping only for three minutes.
Then strain and use that as a mouthwash.
Do not swallow, allow it to swish within the mouth
    holding it in place for a minimum of thirty two seconds.
If there are no open sores, you may also
    use as an alternative to the tea one drop oil of pure peppermint
    in two cups water and follow the same procedure,
    for the same amount of time.

100 The flower of the phlox,
    five petals thrice daily, warmed in the palms of the hand,
    you may ingest until you have ease of pain of the mouth.
This is efficacious for any disease of the mouth.

101 The leaves of the strawberry placed underneath the tongue
    and allowed within the saliva to loose its properties
    will be most efficacious for mouth ulcers,
    of diseases affecting the gums.
You need only five leaves.
Held underneath the tongue for a period of ten minutes,
    swallowing the saliva as it is produced,
    inhibits the further growth of the bacteria
    causing the mouth ulcers.
Placed five times daily, this will then not only alleviate
    and stop the growth,
    but begin to eliminate the bacteria causing that problem.

102 We would speak on the benefits of the orange tree.
And it matters not whether the tree is in the outdoors and is huge,
    or whether it is within the home and is a much smaller version,
    for its properties remain the same.
You have been told of the benefits of the vitamin C
    that is found in abundance within an orange.
You have also been told of the benefits
    of the white flesh of the orange.

We would first caution that all fruit and vegetables be cleansed
     before imbibing, before ingesting into your being.
For when the ground becomes polluted
     then all foods have within them dregs of those pollutants.
Souls of earth, the bark of the orange tree is little used for any remedies.
We would have you know beneath the bark
     is a sap that is efficacious for the healing of canker sores.
It is not the acidity that you associate with the actual orange
     for to put the orange juice upon a canker sore is very painful.
But beneath the bark is a small bit of sap that will soothe the canker sore
     especially within the mouth area, but anywhere upon the body.
You need only one drop of the sap three times daily
     until the canker has disappeared.
This will soothe and stimulate the body's immune system to heal.
You need only take a small bit of shaving with a sharp knife.
No more than two centimeters is necessary.
Take what you need and then push the bark back in place and tie upon it,
     and tie upon it
          a bandage of sorts, a ribbon, it matters not.
This is so the tree itself is not injured and it will gradually heal itself.
Whether the tree is in the environment outside,
     or whether it was within inside, the same small amount is enough.

103   The pure spearmint is soothing for any disease or ailment,
     irritation of the tongue and the mouth, even unto the upper throat.
Pure spearmint, a little dab on the corner of the mouth in a liquid form
     will assist the colicky babe, more so than the pure peppermint.
If you have no oil of pure spearmint,
     the leaf crushed between the fingers
     until you have some moisture,
     and then place on the side of the lips of the mouth,
     so that instinctively the tongue rubs that.
Keep doing that, Soul, until there is no more moisture left in the leaf.
This will help the babe.

104   The vanilla bean in its pure state
     has a variety of efficacious remedies.
We do not recommend the outer covering in any remedy.
It is important to remove the outer shell
     and use only the internal matter.

Crushed[16] into a fine powder, may be used as a remedy
>   for internal sores of the mouth area
>   known as ulcers and cold sores.

For the cold sores, a simple dab is all that is necessary.
To use internally as mouthwash, one teaspoon mixed in half glass water
>   and then rinsed in the mouth,
>   held in the mouth without swallow for twenty three seconds.

You may do this three times each day.

105 The outer bark of the holly tree,
>   a small one by one inch square placed
>   within one fourth cup water,
>   and allowed to sit for three days.

At the end of the three days you will have a soothing medicament
>   for cold sores.

The water may be placed upon cold sores.

106 The juniper bark before it has been dried
>   is useful for the pain of the teeth.

Placed on the outer edge of the jaw in the area
>   of where the tooth or teeth are in pain
>   and held there until the pain recedes.

Within the bark, what you see as moisture
>   is in actuality a healing balm
>   that will penetrate the skin.

In severe cases, where the tooth is infected,
>   the outer bark is cleared away.

The inner bark is then placed inside the mouth upon the afflicted teeth
>   and held in place until the pain recedes.

You will ensure there are no sharp edges before placing it in the mouth.

107 The inner portion of the pine bark
>   placed upon the outer cheek for any tooth swelling,
>   will help reduce the swelling.

The bark may be gently placed within
>   and held in place against the infected tooth.

This will help draw out any infection.

---

16 crushed - do not crush in aluminum or with aluminum

108 We would suggest salal is useful
    to stimulate the production of saliva within a dry mouth.
Chewing of one or two leaves will assist.
This is helpful, Soul, when water is in short supply.

Facial
109 Take the fresh petals of the pansy,
    three petals in each hand is all that is required.
Knead the petals until you feel the moisture,
    then rub on the face.
It will be an astringent,
    cleansing the pores and assisting in the healing of acne.

110 The inner portion of the apple blossom
    is most efficacious for those beings who have roseola, rosea.
Take and rub between your fingers and thumb
    the inner portion of the apple blossom.
This is most efficacious
    for those beings who have roseola, rosea,
        upon the face, even unto the neck.
Gently place it upon, smooth it in, and allow it to sit for fifteen minutes.
And then, gently wipe it away in an upward motion.
Place it on in a downward motion, and lift it off in an upward motion.

111 We would discuss pressure points.
Place the thumbs and the forefingers together
    and the other fingers close together.
Holding in an upright position underneath the chin
    the right hand and the left hand,
    will assist in the calming of painful jaw.
Whether the pain in the jaw is from a dislocation
    or from the teeth or the gums, this will help,
    for it will focus the mind and the Energy upon the jaw.
You will hold it until the pain recedes.

112 Souls, the seed of the star anise is a potent, powerful aid
    in the healing of the disease cancer.
Especially, Souls, the cancer within the face, within the mouth,
    within the throat, within the brain, within the ears,
    within the eyes and within the bones of the head area.

The seeds may be taken on the tongue and allowed to sit upon the tongue
> for a period of three to five minutes.

We recommend, generally, ten of these seeds at one dosage.

This may be repeated three times each day until improvement.

And then the dosage can be decreased to two times a day
> for ten days after notice of improvement.

The healing is best for the star anise seeds within the head area.

It would not be as efficacious for cancers in other parts of the body.

Throat

113   The petals of the deep purple clematis may be dried.

Grind them up to form the powder,
> mix with one quarter cup of olive oil to one tablespoon of powder.

For those developing goiter, cancer of the throat,
> this powder concoction in the early stages,
>> daily rubbed into the flesh and then a scarf placed around the neck
>> for a minimum of two hours each time, done thrice daily,
>> will impede the growth of the cancer and the goiter.

114   You will understand, that the varieties of pansies
> grow differently in different parts of your world,
> but all have the same basic chemical composition
> and all except for the white will assist in a variety of ailments.

The petals of the pansy when placed upon the tongue
> will assist those who have a cough that is phlegmish,
> the cough caused by the drip from the nose,
> the cough caused by the congestion in the chest;
> three petals in their initial state placed upon the tongue
> and held upon the tongue for one minute.

In their dried state, use double the amount.

115   We would have you understand the color purple
> abounds upon your earth
> in plants, trees, indeed even crystals.

You have within nature many examples of this color
> in all varying shades.

It is, Souls of earth, a powerful color.

It is one that is worth study; to study
> the varying plants and flowers and natural occurrences of this color.

All plants that have this color contain healing properties,
>   some very minute and some great.

We would have you understand that within the darker shades,
>   unto a dark shade of purple, one that has depth within it,
>   is most efficacious to place upon the external throat,
>   for the relief of coughs, for the relief of sore throats,
>   for the relief even unto croup.

You do not require more than a few leaves or petals.
You do not need to concoct, to press, to grind.
The leaf in its pure state will be sufficient.
Allow it to absorb the negativity.
In some cases you will even notice a change in color
>   as it absorbs and loses its luster, its depth.

You may place the leaf in its pure state upon the area of the heart
>   to soothe the sore lungs, to help ease the inflammation.

The leaves are to be placed in a straight line starting
>   from the base of the throat all the way unto the navel.

Simply lay them flat and allow the healing to occur.

116 The droppings from your cedars,
>   we would have you understand, they have a use.

Take a half cup of these fallen brown needles,
>   place them in boiling water, steep for five minutes minimum.

Strain and allow the strained water to cool[17].
What you have, Soul, is a tea that is useful
>   for clearing the phlegm from a cold or allergies.

The strained portion is not to be fully ingested.
You will take one teaspoon, place within six ounces of water,
>   and then sip until it is gone.

The sipping allows the chemical to react with the body.
Drinking it quickly does not allow the intermingling
>   with the tongue, the saliva, the throat, and the esophagus.

117 Within each genus of trees there are healing properties.
We would speak upon the healing properties of the pine.
The dried bark, scraped and ground into fine powder, mixed with water
>   and purified is efficacious in the assisting of coughing up of phlegm.

---

17 cool - the boiling water must be slowly brought to cooling,
to room temperature.

The powder, one half teaspoon mixed within one pint water,
> for it is powerful, ingested, one tablespoon every hour
> until the cough ceases bringing up the phlegm.

It is not necessary for more than five hours at maximum
> in even the most desperate of cases.

118 We would ask that every other day for ten days
> you intake one small orange, the whole orange except for the peel.

The white inner part of the peel is especially efficacious when
> you are attempting to heal any condition that encourages phlegm.

And we would ask that for those ten days
> you refrain from all dairy products and then you may resume.

We would ask that you stimulate your digestive tract
> by using a bit of cayenne spice in the food,
> > one eighth teaspoon per day.

This may be cooked or it may be raw.

119 When the plant has reached the height of three feet,
> you may begin to utilize the leaves of the evening primrose.

The leaves of the evening primrose may be used
> for those who have phlegm within the throat.

In that particular case, the leaf must be more than one and a half inches.

Place underneath the tongue,
> and allow the saliva to extract from the leaf the healing of properties.

And after twenty five seconds
> you may remove the leaf from underneath the tongue,
> and proceed to eat it if you wish.

Doing this twice a day will calm the phlegm within the throat.

Neck

120 This is most efficacious for those beings
> who have difficulties with the neck and the shoulders.

Soul, you will understand pressure points.

It is the combination, the triad.

The pressure points and the chemical action
> with the molecular structure of the cells
> > that will penetrate,
> > affect the meridians that flow through your being.

Clear meridians equal clear thinking, clear bodily functions,
> clarity within all that you do.

When the meridians are blocked energy,
> it is as a bottle that has a cork in it
> and as you shake the liquid with your fizz
> the gas builds up and may explode,
> at the very least causes a pressure.

So it is within your meridians, when they are blocked the pressure builds
> and must be released in some manner or form.

And so, clear meridians is often a goal.
We will begin with the meridian in the center of the back of your hands.
That meridian, Soul, is particular to stress and strain
> and injury of the neck, of the shoulders and the upper arms.

Begin with the right hand and finish with the left hand.
Use the finger next to the smallest finger on your hand,
> it is placed upon the point above the third knuckle.

Then, the next finger placed also upon this area.
The two are then held, pressured.
Not, Soul, damaging pressure but a firm pressure
> until you feel the pulse begin.

When the pulse begins you may release the fingers,
> for you have cleared the beginning of that meridian.

You will feel a warmth enter in to the shoulder,
> the upper arm and onto the neck.

Each hand is to be done equally.
After the feeling begins, you will place the finger next to the index finger
> upon the tip of the thumb and you will hold it for a count of three.

Then take a breath and release.
This is to seal for a period of time
> the clarity that you have given to that meridian.

You may repeat as often as necessary.
It is allowed that you continue
> until you have found the relief you desire.

121 The combination of the blue and the purple pansies
> is efficacious for breaks of the neck and the spinal area.

Take five each of the whole flowers and grind them until they separate.
Once they have separated, place one tablespoon of water in the bowl
> along with one eighth teaspoon of salt.

It may be sea salt or ground salt.
Let that sit, for a period of forty five minutes.
And then grind again until you have a paste.

Do not be concerned about the salt.
Leave it as is.
If it is not fully dissolved, that is acceptable.
Place that paste directly upon the broken area.
Pressing very lightly the broken area for as long as you are able,
> but a minimum of twelve minutes.

You may place bandage to hold it in place
> or you may simply hold it in your hand.

This will reduce the swelling
> and stimulate the healing of the broken area.

122   For neck pain caused by stress and tension.
A small ball of beeswax, approximately
> the size that would fit into the palm of a child's hand,
> rolled into a form of a ball.

Place it upon the back of your neck, and gently roll it for neck pain.
It will soothe and relax the muscles.

123   We would provide for you stretching exercises,
> for the health and well being of body and mind.

To stimulate from the neck to the top of the head,
> bring your head to an upright position,
> and then slowly bring it down as far as you are able,
> until you feel the neck begin to stretch.

As far as possible, your back is straight,
> your hands held directly out in front of you, palm down.

And you will feel the stretching of your upper neck and skull.
Once you have reached the stretching, Souls, bring it slowly back up.

Upper Torso

Hands

124 For breaks of the fingers, use the yellow pansies.
Take five of the whole flowers,
    and grind them until they separate.
Once they have separated you will place
    one tablespoon of water in the bowl
    along with one eighth teaspoon of salt.
It may be sea salt or ground salt.
Let that sit for a period of forty five minutes.
And then grind again until you have a paste.
Do not be concerned about the salt.
Leave it as is.
If it is not fully dissolved, that is acceptable.
Place that paste directly upon the broken area.
Pressing very lightly
    the broken area for as long as you are able,
    but a minimum of twelve minutes.
You may place bandage to hold it in place
    or you may simply hold it in your hand.
This will reduce the swelling
    and stimulate the healing of the broken area.

125 This remedy of twelve rosemary needles, the geranium one drop,
    the lavender one drop in warm, not hot water,
    will be sufficient to ease hands that have worked diligently
    throughout a period of time and have become sore and tense.
You may plunge them into the warmed water.

126 For the achy arthritis hands,
   you would require at least twenty five petals of the flower
   and twenty five needles picked at the time of the blossom,
   the geranium one drop and lavender one drop in warm, not hot water.
To ease hands plunge them into the warmed water.
Allow them to sit in warm water
   for a period of twelve minutes.

127 We would suggest, for beings whose hands have become distorted
   due to rheumatoid arthritis, who find it painful to move the hands,
   that to take the inner portion of the banana peel
   and rub it into all portions of the hands, especially in between
   the fingers and between the thumb and the finger.
Allow it to stay upon the skin for two minutes
   before you wipe it away.

128 To ease a carpal tunnel,
   we would suggest ten rosemary needles soaked in the warm water,
   one drop geranium, one drop rosemary oil, and one drop lavender.
And then plunge the hands into the water until you feel ease,
   until feeling begins to return.
For severe cases of this carpal tunnel,
   you may be required to do this three times in an evening
   depending upon the amount of activity during your work period.

129 We would continue with the carpal tunnel.
We would have you make a poultice that you would wrap around the wrist.
The poultice would contain half a teaspoon mustard,
   one drop rosemary, one drop lavender
   in a base of olive oil, one tablespoon.
Place this upon a soft cloth.
Heat it slightly until it is gently warm.
Then you will place around the wrist
   and leave it upon the wrist until it cools.
It may be warmed up thrice.
Each time, it is to be placed upon both wrists,
   even if you do not have an affected one on the other wrist.
There must be a balance.
For it will travel up the shoulder unto the neck.
All is connected.

130 We give unto you an exercise for carpal tunnel.
This is to be done, Souls, three times each day
> until your pain has ceased to exist
> and you may move your wrist
> and fingers and shoulders without pain.

Step 1
Sit straight in a chair, feet on the floor if possible.

Step 2
Rest the edge of the palms upon a surface
> so that your palms are facing each other but not touching.

Step 3
Bring inward the fingers of the left hand, not quite closing as a fist,
> the thumb will rest on top of the forefinger.

Step 4
You will then do the same to the right hand.
Bring the fingers in, but not quite making a fist,
> the thumb resting on top of the forefinger.

Step 5
Lift up your right hand
> approximately six inches off the table,
> and turn over your left hand
> so that the inside of the wrist is upright.

Step 6
Place the right hand with the folded fingers
> on top of the wrist of the left hand.

Step 7
And use the knuckles to knead the wrist.
You will not cause yourself intense pain.
You will only press to the point where the pain begins.
And you will continue to knead with the knuckles
> back and forth upon the wrist for a period for fifteen seconds.

Step 8
You will then stop,
> deep breath, hold for a count of three and release.

Step 9
Move your right knuckles away from the left wrist
> and place the left wrist back in its position in Step 3.

Step 10
Move your right wrist so that it is facing upward.
Take the knuckles of the left hand and begin to knead the
> inside of the right wrist.

Again, Souls, you do not need to harm yourself.
You will knead as tenderly or as deeply as you are able
> and you will continue back and forth upon the wrist
>> for a period for fifteen seconds.

Step 11
Place both hands back into their original position.
You will then, Soul, take the first two fingers of the right hand
> and place them in the middle of the inside of the left wrist.

Bring them with a slight pressure on the skin
> up unto the crook of the elbow,
> and then down to the wrist, maintaining a touch on the arm.

And then, once more up and down.
Apply slight pressure as you are doing this.

Step 12
Take the first two fingers of the left hand
> and place them in the middle of the inside right wrist.

Bring them with a slight pressure on the skin
> up unto the crook of the elbow,
> and then down to the wrist, maintaining a touch on the arm.

And then, once more up and down.
Apply slight pressure as you are doing this.

Step 13
Intertwine the fingers
> place the thumbs on top of the forefingers.

Step 14
Five times, while maintaining the intertwining of the fingers,
> open and close the palms.

Step 15
Move the fingers apart from each other,
> place your palms up and you are finished.

Arms
131 For breaks of the ulna, use the yellow pansies.
Take five of the whole flowers and grind them until they separate.
Once they have separated,
> you will place one tablespoon of water in the bowl
> along with one eighth teaspoon of salt.

It may be sea salt or ground salt.
Let that sit for a period of forty five minutes.
And then grind again until you have a paste.
Do not be concerned about the salt.
Leave it as is.
If it is not fully dissolved, that is acceptable.
Place that paste directly upon the broken area.
Pressing very lightly
> the broken area for as long as you are able,
> but a minimum of twelve minutes.

You may place bandage to hold it in place
> or you may simply hold it in your hand.

This will reduce the swelling
> and stimulate the healing of the broken area.

132 For those confined to the chair
> who experience pain in the upper arms or the lower arms
> we would recommend, Souls of earth,
> the application of the olive oil remedy[18]
> with the addition of one drop eucalyptus oil.

Especially for those who find themselves with the pain
> in the hands and the wrist, daily three times daily,

---

[18] In one quarter cup olive oil will be placed three drops oil of lavender, one drop oil of rosemary, one drop oil of geranium.

across, not up and down, across the wrist
and in a circular motion apply the remedy.

133   To those who have muscular problems of the arm,
the elbow and the shoulder, we suggest the application
of the remedy of one quarter cup olive oil
two drops pure peppermint
upon the pulse of the wrist,
and one inch on either side the inner joint of the elbow,
and underneath the toes,
Gently massage it in.
In all cases you do not require great amounts of the remedy.
A dab will do.
It is important to awaken the body to the need for the balance.

Back
134   We would speak with you on osteoporosis.
We would speak with you on the porosity of the bone density.
We would have you understand the properties of silica
    as an adjunct to the restoration of bone density.
Silica is found in many varieties upon the earth.
A minute portion is all that is necessary daily until improvement is noted,
    until the body feels the strength returning
    and the bones feel almost heavy.

135   There are, Soul, two pressure points
    at the very top of the shoulder blades.
This will alleviate the arthritic pain.
You will feel with your thumb a small indentation that is loose, not firm.
Take your thumbs and gently massage in a clockwise movement,
    eight times on both sides, and then in the very center of the area.
Then move upward with the thumb
    a centimeter into the center of the back of the neck,
    and again in a clockwise movement,
    move your thumb clockwise eight times.

136   The yellow sedum is most efficacious
    for the beings who have difficulty with limbs,

be it arthritic or be it rheumatoid, be it spinal injury,
    any that is affected through the spinal area unto the rest of the being.
Take the sedum, enough to cover and mix it with a bit of olive oil,
    place upon a warm cloth, and fold over the cloth.
The poultice in this case, is to be placed upon the spine.
It will lay upon the back
    for a minimum of thirty three minutes.
Ensure the cloth is warm, but not hot, Souls.
And wherever the pain is at its utmost,
    either the hip or some part of the leg
    or some part of the arm or hand, the neck or the shoulder,
    then a bandana with the sedum inside will be worn upon that area
    so that throughout the day the soothing will be present.
This will assist the being to control the pain throughout the day.
Also, for those beings sorely afflicted in the limbs, we would suggest
    taking of five florets, air drying, grinding into a fine powder.
One tablespoon of the powder per quart of water mixed well
    and divided into fours.
And then, for four days, one quarter each day
    it is sipped gently throughout the day.
And this may be repeated every four days until the pain subsides.

137 For those who suffer from a blow to the spine
    that h as not broken the bone, but has certainly injured it,
    placing the branch of the juniper,
    one that would reach the length of the spine,
    and holding it in place for a period of twenty four hours
    will alleviate the swelling caused by the injury and the pain thereof.

138 For those beings who have spinal injuries,
    we would recommend that the feet be cared for daily;
    four times daily, each time for thirty seconds.
The massage will be done with one quarter cup olive oil,
    one drop of stimulating geranium oil
    and one drop stimulating eucalyptus oil.
Particular attention will be paid to the digits, all the toes.
Each toe is to be gently pulled as it is massaged,
    and then massaged in a circular motion.

And complimenting at the base of the neck from the shoulder
> to the very tip of the spinal column, massage will be done
> with the same ingredients in a circular motion for thirty seconds.

Both hands will be used in the circular massage.
This will provide stimulus and balance.

139 We would have you understand,
> for those beings who have great difficulty with the spinal corridor,
> there is a technique to assist in clearing the spinal corridor.

Step 1
Slightly cup your dominant hand,
> whether it be right or left.

The other hand rests upon a surface,
> your feet flat on the ground or towards the ground.

Thumb closed against the flesh.

Step 2
Slightly bend your head forward.

Step 3
Take the four fingers of the dominant hand
> and place above the beginning of the neck.

This is your neck corridor.

Step 4
Palpate the neck firmly, not so that you will hurt yourself,
> but so that you can hear.

Palpate once, twice, thrice, stop.
Rest your fingers.
Palpate once, twice, thrice, stop
Rest your fingers.
Palpate once, twice, thrice, stop.
Rest your fingers.

Step 5
Bring your head slightly up,
> and again, palpate once, twice, thrice, stop,
> hold for the count of seven and then release.

Step 6
Slowly, Soul, very slowly, raise the head upright.

140   A person suffering from backache, not due to disease,
        but only due to overwork, to slight injury,
        may find it effective to notice the feet ache also.
The bottom of the feet, Soul, will often be an indication
        of the back being out of alignment.
We would suggest the placing the massage unto three areas of the foot:
        the area of the large toe, the toe itself and the sole beneath,
        the area of the little toe and the area beneath, and the heel.
Each area to be massaged gently with the olive oil,
        one quarter cup with one drop pure peppermint oil.
This will bring back a balance and ease the ache.

141   This will bring blood and healing to the shoulder,
        it will stimulate the healing for the back.
Sit in a firm chair,
        place the hands in the prayer position.
Bring the hands as far as possible,
        without pain to the right, without moving the torso,
        and hold for a count of five.
After a count of five, bring the hands into the center,
        hold them for the count of five.
Then bring the hands as far as possible,
        without pain to the left, without moving the torso
        and hold for the count of five.
Now bring the hands back to the center for the count of five.
You will do this exercise thrice each time
        and you will do it three times a day.

142   For that hunched over pain and stiffness,
        hold your neck upright and make a fist with both hands.
Bring the fists together so that the knuckles touch
        and push in so that you feel it along the back of your shoulders.
Hold for the count of five seconds,
        then move your hands away.
Again bring the fists together so that the knuckles touch
        and push in so that you feel it along the back of your shoulders.

Hold for the count of five,
> then move your hands away.

Once more bring the fists together so that the knuckles touch
> and push in so that you feel it along the back of your shoulders.

Hold for the count of five,
> then move your hands away.

143   For the pain of the back:

Step 1
Place olive oil within the hands.

Step 2
You will then place palms flat upon the scapula of both sides of the back.

Step 3
Ten times in a clockwise motion,
> gently massage both sides at the same time.

You will not use great pressure.

Step 4
Slowly bring the palms toward each other, meeting at the center.

Step 5
Move the flat palms with slight pressure down the center of spine
> onto the tail bone where you will move your palms apart
> > on either side of the spine.

Step 6
Placing palms flat, gently massage upward,
> all the way over the tops of the shoulder.

Step 7
At the tops of the shoulders, ten times in a clockwise motion,
> gently massage both sides at the same time.

Step 8
Move the palms inward to the neck area
> and bring your fingers down the center spine
> > finishing at the tail bone and releasing.

144 To strengthen the lower back,
Each day take five minutes to sit in a comfortable chair
    and do the following exercises.
All this is to be done very slowly.

Step 1
Place your hands palms up in your lap.

Step 2
Slowly, very slowly,
    raise them until they have reached the heart level.

Step 3
When they have reached the heart level,
    move them outward from the elbow,
    not from the shoulder, as far as you are able.
And hold that position for fifteen seconds
    ensuring that your spine is straight
    and your head is in the neutral position,
    neither up or down, or back or to the side.

Step 4
At the end of the fifteen seconds, you will feel movement
    in your lower back, of warmth.
Then bring your hands back together,
    still the palms up, back to the heart level.

Step 5
Bring the palms to your lap.

Step 6
When they are again resting up on your lap,
    we would have you ensure your spine is straight.
And then move only your head down as far as it will go
    and hold it for a count of six seconds.
And then slowly bring it back upright.
At any time, if you feel dizzy, stop, wait for the dizziness to pass.
    and then continue bringing your head back up.

145 Do this daily, Soul, as often as you wish
       and you will find a strengthening of your back.
At no time allow pain.
Each day sit in a straight back chair,
       one where your feet may be flat upon the ground.

Step 1
Do not sit back against the chair at this point,
       merely sit as straight as possible.

Step 2
Place the palms of your hand upon the thighs of your being.

Step 3
Bring the neck upward, raise your chin but not to the point of pain.
Hold the chin in a non pain position for seven seconds.

Step 4
Bring the chin down and move it to your left as far as you are able.
Hold for seven seconds.

Step 5
Bring the chin back into the center, maintaining
       your palms upon your thighs
       and your back as straight as possible.

Step 6
Move the chin as far as possible to the right
       and hold for seven seconds.

Step 7
Bring the chin back into the center.
Take a deep breath and let it out slowly, gently.

Step 8
Relax back so that your back is now touching the back of the chair.
Breathe slowly and deeply for another two minutes
       holding your palms flat on your thighs.

Heart

146   Arteries clogged with plaque can be cleansed with combination:
      mix one teaspoon fresh ground fine rosemary,
      with one teaspoon pure olive oil, not diluted,
      and add a pinch of saffron.
Take internally, do not heat.
Take internally two times each day, six days.
Restrict intake of fat,
      restrict intake of flesh six days.
Restrict intake of caffeine, six days.
Intake profuse amounts of water daily,
      six glasses twice daily, six days.
Treatment once yearly if intake of flesh resumes.

147   We would speak upon your goji berries.
We will tell you, Soul, what we know.
We would recommend, for a remedy, you are to take the skin,
      for therein lies the majority of the nutrients of this berry.
The skin is most efficacious for the heart;
      various types of heart problems
      where the arteries have become clogged,
      where the arteries have become flaccid,
      where the muscles of the heart have become flaccid,
      where there is infection of the heart,
      the surrounding area close to,
      including the neck and below to the navel.
This area, Souls of earth, can be helped by the ingestion of the goji skin.
Five skins, placed in the mouth, under the tongue,
      for a period of a minimum of sixty three seconds.
The saliva will be enhanced with the properties of the goji skin.
It will cause the being to salivate.
And swallowing that saliva will bring into the body the remedy.
After the sixty three seconds, Soul, you may eat the skins.
Skins may be dried for future use or ingested as is in their raw state.
In either case no cooking, no heat is to be applied to the skins.
For ease of swallowing, in many cases, the dried will be the better solution.
If the powder is dry it must be for the adult,
      one half teaspoon ingested once per day,
          sprinkled on a bit of food, not cooked.

For the child up to the age of fifteen, one eighth teaspoon will suffice.
To dry the skins, you will place them upon a natural surface,
    not man made, in a cool dry area,
    and allow them to be covered with a natural cloth,
    but one that is absorbent so that the liquid may be absorbed.
When they have dried,
    you may then place them in a glass container with a cloth covering
    so that air is allowed in and out,
    but not dirt.
The cloth is to be natural.
The dried skin of the goji berry may be kept within a cool area, shaded,
    for up to three months.
In areas where refrigeration is possible they may be kept up to six months.
We would suggest where there is no refrigeration,
    that the jar be placed within the ground,
    with the top portion of the glass sticking up but shaded.
And this will also serve to keep it for three months.

148 Souls, you will understand the heart is a fragile
    and yet amazingly strong organ.
It, too, is affected by many factors.
The general remedy for the heart attack
    which is the gradual increase of walking where applicable
    or the gradual increase of activity, exercises,
    whether the person is ambulatory or confined.
It is important to invigorate the system.
The deep green vegetables are of importance.
The external dark green squash is of the green vegetable
    but in the case of squash, any type is acceptable.
The oatmeal is of importance and the refraining from flesh is advisable,
    for the system is made to work harder when you ingest the flesh.
We do not say one hundred percent abstention,
    but we do advise minimal amounts per week of any flesh.
Soul, whether it be the beef, liver of any animal, the flesh of fish,
    we would recommend no more than two ounces per day.
That is maximum.
Eggs, in the addition of eight per week, are acceptable.

149 Alternate treatment for heart problem.
Indeed, there is an alternative.

HOLISTIC HEALING

The primary alternative is to heal with the Essence of your being.
You can, Soul!
Indeed, you can.
And we would say to you, enter, reach unto Essence,
    allow and know the healing has taken place.
That is always the primary healing of any being;
    to allow healing from the sacred self,
    the Essence of your being,
    the Light of Creator to flow
    within each and every cell of your being,
    bringing it back to the perfection of wellness.
We have a further alternative.
We do not say to you:
    "Refuse the surgery, refuse the bypass, refuse the hospital."
Soul, that is your choice.
We can only offer you another remedy.
We would have you refrain from all meat,
    not just for a moment, but for all time upon your earth.
Also refrain from all sugars except for honey.
Refrain from all refined flours in any form.
Refrain from all wheat.
Refrain from caffeine.
This is not a one time regiment of eating.
It is to be maintained throughout or the problem will reoccur.
Refrain from stress.
Daily, Soul, three times daily, meditate
    and allow healing to enter in,
    allow tranquillity to enter in,
    allow peace.
Refrain from fear during the meditations.
The three times daily may be each time
    for a ten to twenty minute period.
We would also have you daily rock your being.
This is to be done after the meditations.
It is to be done for a three minute period.
You do not require a rocker.
You may simply rock your being in a chair.
We would have you walk
    minimum of thirty five minutes, daily.

This may be broken up into shorter periods of time
> as long as it totals the thirty five minutes per day.

And the walking must be as vigorous as you can,
> in order to generate
>> the adrenalin through your system in a positive manner.

We are partial to marching to invigorate the being.
You may march and walk at the same time.
This too is to be done every day.
If there is a particular impediment to walking every day,
> upon that day attempt to exercise in your chair.

Understand in the beginning this may seem difficult
> but as you continue you will build up your strength.

We have to tell you, Soul, that all choice is yours.
It will take great strength of will in order to perfect an earth alteration.
It takes only acceptance to affect an alteration from your sacred self.
It is choice.
We can not take from you the burden of choice.

150 Souls, we will speak now on the properties of the iris.
The bud is plucked, not cut, plucked and peeled.
Do not crush the bud or flatten it.
It must be peeled gently, for strenuous ripping will decrease potency.
Once you have peeled a complete bud,
> you may mix all parts of the bud together with olive oil.

The olive oil is only used as a containment and to penetrate.
The mixture is to be left in the air for a minimum
> of one and a half hours before application.

It may be ingested as is or it may be placed upon cold foods.
Placed upon a hot dish will remove the potency.
For those who have stroke and are in the recovery stages of stroke,
> one half teaspoon once daily will assist the brain to heal,
>> to replace, to replenish the damage caused
>>> by the disruption of the stroke.

151 This will assist a being who has a heart rate that is out of control.
You call them palpitations.
At the first bloom of the purple iris, pluck the whole head of the flower.
Hold it in your hand and rub until it becomes a gooey mass.
> and it has absorbed some of the energy of your hand.

Place it upon the chest and
> hold the mass with the hand upon the chest
> for a full five minutes.

At the end of the five minutes you may remove the gooey mass.

152 We would discuss pressure points.
We would have you understand
> placing together the thumb and the forefinger,
> and pressing the pads of the thumb and the forefinger
> have a direct relationship unto the brain.

The left thumb and forefinger pressed together
> affects that side of the brain;
> the right thumb and forefinger pressed together
> affects the right side.

You do not crisscross, Soul.
And we would have you understand that the position of the hands,
> with the thumb and the forefingers pressed,
> makes a difference in the position of the other fingers,
> and the way the hand is held.

To calm palpitations, hold the hands thus;
> thumbs and forefingers pressed together,
> the other three fingers pressed closely together,
> and the hand held not upright but facing
> unto the area of the heart.

Hold close to the flesh,
> pressing the thumb and the forefinger and releasing
> take a deep breath, and you will notice
> a relaxation of the palpitations.

Lungs

153 Into the center gradation of a yellow, still light,
> but no trace whatsoever of white,
> and with the slight deepening of color,
> worn by those who have diseases of the lung
> will assist in giving some breath, ease of breath to that being.

Band the chest with this color, at least six inches in width.
This is to be worn in extreme cases throughout the day, each day.
In those cases where the disease is beginning,
> where there is only asthmatic shortness of breath,

one hour three times daily will suffice
to give some ease to the breathing.

154 We will speak upon brown sedum
and we speak of the flowering heads.
The brown is efficacious when made into a poultice.
You will need enough to cover the chest of the being.
For those who have the tuberculosis or the lung disease caused by mining,
this is most efficacious.
The poultice is to be placed upon the being
for a minimum of thirty one minutes.
Take the sedum, enough to cover and mix it with a bit of olive oil,
place upon a warm cloth, and fold over the cloth
so that it lays upon the chest.
There will be a small aromatic
they will inhale which will help the breathing.
It will soothe and calm the breathing,
enabling the being to take a little deeper breath.
It also would be most efficacious to wear upon the neck area
a cloth similar to the one placed upon the chest
with the sedum inside and wrap as a kerchief,
a bandana around the neck, so that throughout the day
the soothing will be present.

155 The remedy for walking pneumonia
consists of the inhalation of eucalyptus oil.
This is to be placed near but not directly at the side of the patient.
It will be placed within twenty four inches.
The oil is not to be lit, it is only to be loosed into the air.
Once daily a waft across the nostrils.
Not directly in the nostrils, but waft across the nostrils.
We also advise those with the chest congestion
to use the mustard.
The poultice is comprised of one teaspoon of prepared mustard.
Place within the mustard one drop rosemary, one drop lavender.
Spread one third of this concoction thinly upon a wet cloth on the back.
No more than five minutes each time.
The end of five minutes remove cloth, dry yourself,
wait fifteen minutes, use another one third of the concoction.

Same procedure, remove, dry yourself and then proceed to last third.
And we would suggest the legs to be placed up
> at a forty five degree angle in the evening before sleep.

This will assist in the constriction,
> elevation of the constriction of the body,
> for all the body is involved in fighting any illness.

Placed upon the feet before raising the legs,
> will be olive oil, one tablespoon
> with one drop of rosemary and one drop of geranium.

This is to be gently rubbed into the soles of the feet
> and it will be absorbed into the system.

The patient needs to understand
> that this remedy we advise will take a time.

It will not provide relief in the matter of an instant,
> but it will provide relief and comfort.

We would also suggest, in the severe cases,
> that the full back be rubbed with a concoction consisting of
> the olive oil, the rosemary and the geranium.

And we would have placed here, in the throat area,
> two drops lavender, twice daily.

The back may be rubbed as often as the patient requests for comfort,
> for the warmth will ease the stress.

156 For those people who have difficulty with the breath,
> for those who have the congestion of the lung
> brought about by the irritation of tobacco,
> or the irritation of smoke, of pollution, of toxins,
> it would be efficacious to chew upon a sprig of the spider plant,
> approximately a two to three inch sprig.

It is not necessary to swallow, only to chew, to mash.
You will notice as you chew the saliva will increase,
> and that is your indication,
> that you are removing from the leaf
> the positive chemicals for your well being.

For it is the chemical within the spider plant that expands the bronchi.
Then, Soul, you may spit out.
This will bring breath unto the personage.
For a baby, you will mash, you will chew within your own mouth,
> and give only to the child some of the saliva
> that contains the chemical within.

157   We would have you understand
       the bronchial tubes are sensitive to all manner of toxicity.
They are vulnerable to all manner of emotional upset.
The emotionality of bronchitis
       is the body attempting to spew forth the toxins
       that have built up due to the suppression of emotions
       that are better off released in a positive manner.
The physicality occurs when the suppression reaches a point
       when the body can no longer sustain in wellness.
This is true for all diseases of the lung and the areas around the lungs.
Soul, we would recommend the infusion daily,
       three times daily, of the pure peppermint leaf.
You will take ten leaves, lay them within tepid water for five minutes
       and then slowly heat until just before boiling point.
You will then cool the infusion, separate the leaves from the liquid,
       drink the liquid, three cups per day,
       and chew the pure peppermint leaves, thirty per day.
These are to be the leaves you used to make the infusion.
They will be most pleasant to the passages.
In most cases the pure peppermint will provide the relief that is sought.

158   On a physical level, Soul,
       we would suggest the following course of action for bronchitis.
Each morning after the east ritual[19],
       take in three shallow breaths in quick succession
       and exhale as long as able.
And then breathe normally
       for a minimum of thirty seconds
       and then repeat the inhalation and exhalation just given.
Wait the thirty seconds again
       and for the third time do the breathing exercise.
We would also suggest that once daily a mixture
       of one quarter cup of olive oil with one drop of eucalyptus oil
       and one drop geranium oil be lightly
       massaged along the upper back for three days.
Thereafter, once weekly until the bronchial irritation is gone.
The breathing exercise must be done daily
       to expel from the bronchial tubes
       the irritating membrane that has become infected.

---

19 east ritual – see APPENDIX A

The membranes within the bronchial may indeed be expelled.
Not, Soul, the actual physical representation,
>but the negative energy being held within
>is expelled with this breathing exercise.

The exercise is to be done daily for a period of seven weeks.
Thereafter once weekly for three weeks
>and thereafter once monthly for three months
>and all negative from the bronchial would have been expelled.

159   For those who have access to the baobab tree,
>we would have you understand
>the fruit is efficacious for assisting in breathing difficulties.

The fruit is to be plucked in the morning when there is dew upon the fruit.
It is then, Soul, warmed in the palm of the hand,
>and held one hand over the other with the fruit in the center.

It is to be held for five minutes
>and then the fruit may be crushed within a small dish.

You will have an aroma that as you breathe in deeply
>will assist in opening the bronchial tubes.

For the young infant who can not breathe in deeply,
>hold the bowl near the nostrils, so that as they breathe in,
>they breathe in the efficacious fumes and ease the croupiness,
>the whooping cough, the bronchial infections.

You may effectively keep this concoction
>for a period of sixty one days, preferably in a cool, dark area
>and when it is necessary to use, within that time period
>bring it out and let it warm at room temperature,
>and again the fumes will be released.

160   For congestions, take a handful of juniper leaves,
>place in boiling water.

No more than a quarter cup of leaves
>is necessary for three cups of water.

Stir for one minute
>and then let sit for three minutes and then strain.

The juniper leaves that you have strained out,
>may be retained for a poultice.

Placed within muslin or a cheesecloth, a porous cloth,
>and then placed upon the chest of those who are congested
>and allowed to stay until cool.

This poultice may be used up to three times in that day.
Each time, warmed gently within hot water
> and then strain the water and replace the poultice on cloth
> and place upon the congestion.

The aroma will help also to unclog the sinus.

161 Soul, when you have congestion,
> whether it is within the nasal or within the chest cavity,
> shouting is most efficacious.

You may shout any word, it matters not the word.
What matters is the expansion of the being as you shout the word forth.
This stimulates the nasal passages.
It stimulates within the bronchial chest area.
Shout once every hour until the clearing, the congestion has eased.

162 When the evening primrose plant has reached the height of three feet,
> you may begin to utilize the leaves of the evening primrose,
> the leaves that have reached a growth
> of at least one and a half inches in length.

For those who have persistent cough, dry persistent cough,
> a poultice of the leaves of the evening primrose
> would be most efficacious, warmed not hot,
> upon the chest area for a period of one half hour.

Place within one cup warm water
> three drops olive oil, and a minimum of ten leaves.

Leave the leaves within the water and olive oil
> for a period of one half hour.

The water must be warm not hot.
And at the end of that one half hour,
> take the wet leaves and place them upon a natural cloth
> and then lay that cloth upon the being.

The cloth should be thin
> so that the seepage of the leaves and their medicinal properties
> may enter in to the skin of the being.

163 For the rattling cough we would ask that you
> place upon a thin cloth a small amount of eucalyptus oil.

And then gently warm the cloth and place upon the chest twice daily.
The vapours will assist in ameliorating your distress.
We would ask also that when you retire in the evening

that you place that cloth with the eucalyptus oil upon your back
   and sleep with it so that during the night
   it will also be received.
We would ask further that you place on the bottoms of your feet
   on the soles, a thin line of lavender oil on each.
We would have one more suggestion,
   one quarter teaspoon of fresh rosemary needles
   in any meal during the day.
It is not to be cooked.
It may be ground fine.
This, Soul, is to be done for ten days.

164   The white onion is most efficacious for the croupy cough
   that can not be contained in any other way,
   or when other remedies are unavailable.
Take the onion, white, slice it in half vertically, place it upon the chest,
   cover it, with a cloth and lay in place
   until you hear the cough begin to ease.
The cloth, Soul, is only to prevent the gas of the onion
   from affecting the eyes.

165   The petals of the apple blossom,
   dried and ground into a fine powdery substance,
   mixed with a bit of rosemary.
No more than one eighth teaspoon of rosemary to five full flower petals.
Grind the two together and place within a tea.
Place one quarter teaspoon
   into a cup of tea, stir and slowly sip.
It will soothe the being who has soreness from repeated coughing.
It does not cease the cough, for there are other remedies for that,
   but it does soothe the flesh that has been abused by the coughing.

166   Broken ribs may be helped
   by the combination of the yellow and the purple pansies.
Take five of the whole flowers,
   and grind them until they separate.
Once they have separated, place over them two tablespoons of water
   along with two tablespoons of salt.
It may be sea salt or ground salt.

Let that sit for a period of forty five minutes,
    and then grind again until you have a paste.
Do not be concerned about the salt.
Leave it as is.
If it is not fully dissolved, that is acceptable.
Once ground into a paste,
    place that directly upon the area of the broken rib.
And hold it pressing the broken area very lightly
    for a minimum of twelve minutes.
You may, Soul, place bandage to hold it in place
    or you may simply hold it in your hand.
This will reduce the swelling and stimulate the healing of the broken area.

Lower Torso

Abdomen

167 We would suggest during a pregnancy
  that each day the mother rub gently upon the belly
  in clockwise circles the following:
  one quarter cup olive oil,
  one drop rosemary, one drop geranium oil.
You need not use the full quarter cup, Souls;
  you may use this until it is finished and then replenish.
It need not be slathered on, a light coating is sufficient.
And we would ask that you leave it on,
  for a minimum of twenty minutes
  before wiping off or washing.
This will soothe the skin.
It will penetrate and the very motion, the circular motion clockwise
  sends Energy unto the babe within.
Positive Energy,
  with the focus, the intent of Love and Energy.

168 Sleep for pregnant women.
Soul, for the pregnant woman with trouble at bedtime,
  we recommend marjoram.
We would recommend developing a paste of the powder marjoram
  and a bit of honey, pure honey.
The paste is composed of one quarter teaspoon marjoram
  and enough honey to make the paste.
This may be increased up to one teaspoon if necessary.

169 For the pregnancy in the fifth month,
    rubbing of the inner portion of the banana peel
    upon the outer womb is most efficacious.
It will penetrate through the skin,
    and the vibration of the rubbing, done gently,
    will be most soothing to the child within.

170 The stem of the pansy is most efficacious
    for those diseases of the inners, of the pelvic area in the woman.
It is, Soul, a cleanser for the womb.
It is not to be taken during a pregnancy but after the pregnancy.
The stems of at least three plants are to be sliced up
    and ingested twice daily for three days
    and this will clear the womb.

171 We would speak with you on the properties of pure mint
    and all the cousins of pure mint.
The family of pure mint is extensive, and yet, all have a similar properties.
We would have you know of the pure peppermint.
We would have you understand that a small leaf of pure peppermint,
    chewed or held in the mouth if there is no teeth,
    is efficacious for digestion.

172 Souls, we will speak on the properties of the pure peppermint leaf.
The most efficacious section of the plant is the leaf.
It has long been known to provide a soothing relief
    for ailments of the digestive tract.
But, Souls, we would give you a remedy that is not in common usage.
The processed and the processing of the pure peppermint leaf
    leaves only a small residue of its efficacious properties
    and it adds toxins.
We would have you use fresh pure peppermint leaf.
To receive the most benefit from the pure peppermint leaf,
    it is to be plucked at first dawning.
Any dew found upon the leaf is to be retained.
The leaf may be chewed immediately after the plucking,
    or for future use it may be sun dried
    and allowed to naturally crumble.
When it has crumbled, you may then place it in a glass repository.

A half teaspoon of the crumbled is equal to one fresh leaf.
For mild burnings, irritation, and upset stomach and duodenum,
> three leaves, chewed simultaneously, slowly,
>> so that the juices may mingle with the digestive juices
>> will be sufficient.

For those who have overindulged, who have gastric problems,
> a remedy from six to ten is advisable.

It is imperative that the chewing be done slowly.
The mastication is necessary for the interaction of the internal gastric juices
> in that of the pure peppermint.

173 We would explain to you the properties of clover.
We would have you understand that the clover is most efficacious
> as a digestive aid for not only animals but also for human beings.

You require only one fresh clover.
If it is dried, you will require five.
One clover taken in the mouth and held under the tongue,
> not chewed, simply held under the tongue,
> as your digestive juices will dissolve the healing properties.

It will not dissolve the clover,
> but it will dissolve the properties that will enter into your digestion.

We do not advocate heavy meals, but we do understand
> that you do indulge in such from time to time.

And we would suggest that in order to compensate
> for the overwhelming of your digestion, that you take the clover.

It is important, Souls of earth, that you understand your digestion
> when overwhelmed, ceases to work.

And when it ceases to work you place great strain upon all
> your other organs, not just the stomach, the gallbladder, the liver,
> but there is strain also upon the heart, upon the brain, all.

We can not stress enough the importance of restraining overindulgence
> in food to maintain optimum health, optimum well being.

174 The petals of the apple blossom may be dried and kept.
The petals of five apple blossoms
> dried and ground into a fine powdery substance,
>> mixed with no more than one eighth teaspoon of ground rosemary.

Place one quarter teaspoon into a cup of tea that is palatable to the being
> who has severe stomach indigestion.

Stir and slowly sip, and it will soothe the inners.

175 We would speak on the properties of the periwinkle.
The periwinkle is most efficacious when ground to a fine pulp.
You would use the leaves in this particular instance.
The leaves are to be dried, sun dried, and then ground to a fine powder.
The powder is then mixed with purified water
      in the ratio of half teaspoon of the powder to one quart water,
      for it does not require a great deal of the periwinkle leaves
      in order to be most efficacious.
In the case of the being who has debilitating digestive problems of any sort,
      the daily ingestion of one teaspoon of the periwinkle water
      will assist in bringing the digestion into balance.
For the most severe of cases two teaspoons per day will be sufficient.
You will continue with the one teaspoon per day, in most cases,
      until the body is in balance
      and the digestive problems have been ameliorated.

176 We would speak on the properties of the plantain.
The plantain, Souls of earth,
      is most efficacious when used in its proper cleansing.
It is imperative that the skin be cleansed before it is opened.
The fruit of the plantain contains chemicals
      that are conducive to the digestion.
In this particular case it makes a difference
      as to how the inner plantain fruit is eaten.
Thin slices, minute thin slices,
      no more than two inches long are placed upon the tongue.
Allow the chemicals within to enter in to the tongue
      and thereby into the body.
Allow it to sit upon the tongue for fifteen seconds
      and then you may swallow.
For the efficacy of the fruit of the plantain
      to work its magic upon the digestion,
        it is necessary for the interaction with the saliva.
Depending upon the severity of the indigestion,
      you may require three to five of these thin slices
      to be held upon the tongue.
Not together, individually.
Hold one upon the tongue for fifteen seconds
      and then swallow.
Take the next and repeat as necessary.

You will come to know how many you require
> by the relief you experience
> and how long it takes to experience that relief.

177 We would have you understand that a small leaf of pure peppermint,
> chewed or held in the mouth is efficacious for digestion.

For simple digestion problems, a leaf of pure peppermint after every meal
> will go a long way to ameliorating any disruption of the being.

178 This honey healing is only anathema to the physical human body
> when that contains great toxins.

In areas of intense manufacturing using coal, the honey
> has no healing value for it has been contaminated
> and the contamination, especially in the cases of open burns,
> will enter in and will be of no assistance to the healing.

And so it behooves mankind to be aware
> from where the honey has come from.

You have varying amounts of places where the bees obtain,
> and we would suggest to you, Souls,
> that clover has the most healing properties.

One half teaspoon of honey per day
> greatly enhances the digestive system.

This may be taken first thing in your day;
> whether your day beings in the night or at dawn, it matters not.

The half teaspoon is not to be placed upon or in
> heated liquid of any kind to receive the full benefits.

The very small child under two years of age,
> one eighth teaspoon is all that is required.

Children from two to twelve, one quarter teaspoon.

Thereafter, Soul, half a teaspoon.

And again, Soul, be aware of where you have the honey from.

179 We bring unto you a beneficial sound
> that will stimulate the gastric juices to help in digestion.

Ensure that you remain with thumbs over the third and fourth fingers
> and the third and fourth fingers held closely to each palm.

And then upon a surface,
> you will start with the first two fingers of the right hand
> down on a surface
> and the left raised slightly up

and then bring the left down
and raise the right and bring the right down and raise the left.
And you will ensure that between the raising
of the right and the left and the coming down,
that you allow two earth seconds at least between movements.
Up and down, up and down.
Ensure that you remain with thumbs over the third and fourth fingers
and the third and fourth finger held closely to the palm.
Continue the gentle rhythm
and you will begin to feel within the stomach, a calming.
And you will understand the gastric juices and the digestion
are now being synchronized.
It is important that you are sitting.
If you are not sitting and must lay, then ensure you are as close as possible,
when doing the rhythm, to the stomach area.
For it is the sound that the body reacts to.
And it is the movement that the body reacts to.
And this particular sound and movement affects the digestion.
When you feel a relief begin, place the two fingers
of the right hand intertwined with the left first two fingers,
the left forefinger will be over the right forefinger.
And then you will press gently into your duodenum
and hold for the count of two and then release.
Again, hold for the count of two and release.
Again, hold for the count of two and release.
This will stabilize the action within the digestion.

180 Salal is efficacious for the young child, the baby,
who has distended abdomen, who has stomach cramp.
Placing eight leaves upon the stomach[20] with a bit of olive oil
and wrapping them so that they stay upon the body
for a length of time, assists
in the reduction of the gastric disturbance.
A paste made of four dried, crushed leaves, mixed with the olive oil,
may be placed upon the tongue of the child,
along with some water or some milk, so that the salal enters in.
You need only one eighth teaspoon.

---

20 leaves upon the stomach – arrange in a circular pattern around the navel.

181   A small ball of beeswax,
     approximately the size that would fit
     into the palm of a child's hand, rolled into a form of a ball,
     placed within the top of the navel cavity
     and rolled around will help calm an upset stomach.
It is the action of the rolling that stimulates the juices within.
There are efficacious properties within the beeswax
     that are caught by the flesh of your being.

182   We bring unto you uses of the skin of squash,
     particularly of those squash with the dark green color.
For those, even unto the babe, who have distress of the stomach,
     internal distress of the stomach will abate
     with the application of this on the external of the stomach.
You may grate, scrape, peel the squash,
     until you have a minimum one quarter cup of the skin.
Grind up the skin until the liquid appears, the moisture.
There will not be copious amounts but there will be some,
     and that is the oil that is necessary to the concoction.
Once you have the oil coming to fruition from your grinding,
     you will combine it with the skin,
     and mix in one quarter cup olive oil,
     one drop rosemary and one drop lavender oils.
Allow this to sit in a cool area out of the sun,
     for a period of three hours.
Stir once again the concoction
     and use it to place upon the belly.
It is to be left until the distress abates.
This is most efficacious for the child with colic;
     you may bandage, loose, not with adhesive,
     but swaddle the babe with cloth so that it will be held in.
It is the grinding that brings forth the healing properties.
During the period this is laid upon the stomach, do not ingest cold water.
It is prohibited in order for the healing to occur.
For if your body must react to cold water,
     it takes away the focus of what is occurring in the stomach.
Warm water is acceptable during this process
     but neither cold nor hot is acceptable.

183 The root of the amaranth, sliced thin, a sliver of four inches long,
for the very young roots you may require
four slices to make the four inches,
ground, placed in one third cup of water,
covered and let set for four days.
And, Souls of earth, we would request that at any point in time
you do not use a plastic or metal to hold the concoction.
One half teaspoon to the colicky infant
will soothe the digestion and the irritation within the bowel.
A full teaspoon may be efficacious for the adult
who is having diarrhea cramps
and it will soothe both the intestine and the digestion.

184 For the colicky babe who is in pain and frustrated with the pain,
we would suggest oil of cinnamon,
off to the side, not directly underneath.
Again you may burn it in a diffuser or you may
place the oil upon a cloth and keep it nearby
for fifteen minutes.

185 You may make a tea of the inner portion
and the outer petals of the wallflower.
The tea can only be made at first bloom.
Removing the inner portion and the petals around it,
placing in boiling water for two minutes, makes a tea
that may be placed upon the stomach when cooled
to ease the inner digestion, to ease the colicky babe,
to ease the shooting pains that often are called cramping.
Simply place and allow to dry.

186 We would speak on the properties of the cabbage family;
specifically cabbage, in itself, the red cabbage and the cauliflower.
Both have interchangeable qualities
and so whatever is to hand will be sufficient.
The flower is also of use in powdered form.
And so you would dry it, air dry it.
Remove all moisture and then air dry it until it becomes crumbly
and then grind that into a fine powder.
And this may be ingested.

One teaspoon to one quart of water is all that is necessary
    to assist internally in the healing of gastritis or colic
    of those babes beyond three months.
You only require for the babes, one eighth teaspoon
    and for the adult one teaspoon.
You may refrigerate or keep in a cool dark area the remainder.

187 We would have you know that you may scrape gently
    a bit of the bark of the orange tree
    to the amount of one half teaspoon and place these shavings
    into one quarter cup of water
    and leave it exposed to the air within the water
    for a period of three days.
Then strain from this water the shavings
    and you will have a tincture to assist
    in the calming of a colicky babe,
    to assist in the grippe, the pain caused by flu, by the diarrhea.
It will soothe the inner walls of the stomach
    and the duodenum on into the small intestine.
For a babe under the age of three, one eighth teaspoon every three hours
    is sufficient.
Over the age of three, it will be one half teaspoon for every fifty pounds
    of body weight every three hours if necessary.
But one dose should be sufficient.
It will also assist in reducing fever.
In that respect it is placed directly upon the forehead,
    rubbed into the forehead in addition to the imbibing
    of the dosage previously given.

188 For the babe who is colicky,
    we would have you develop an infusion
    comprised of three parts water to one part pure spearmint,
    so that if you have three tablespoons of water
    you will have one tablespoon pure spearmint leaves.
Then place pure spearmint within the water
    and let sit for a period of no more than six hours.
Once you have the infusion developed,
    you will place the pure spearmint that has been soaked
    directly upon the stomach of the ailing child.

You do not require to cover the stomach;
> an area of three centimeters will be acceptable.

Over the dampened leaves you will place a warm cloth,
> not hot, but warm.

And you will, Soul, hold it lightly
> with the flat of your hand upon the child's stomach.

As soon as the cloth cools, you will warm it again
> and place fresh pure spearmint leaves.

It is not necessary to wash away that which is there, simply place more.
Again, warm the cloth, place the flat of your hand on top.
Do this for fifteen minutes
> or less, should the child cease its agony.

189 For the colicky baby, place the leaves of the green tea
> that have been strained from the liquid
> upon the stomach and gently rub
> with your own hands until the being is soothed.

Green tea is efficacious when cooled.
In the making of the tea use two tablespoons
> of green tea leaves to one cup of water.

The tea is not to be boiled.
It is to be set within hot almost boiling water
> and allowed to sit for ten minutes.

190 For those who have the Crohn's,
> pure spearmint is much better for the system than pure peppermint.

Be careful of your medicaments, your medications
> that contain oil of pure peppermint
> if you have Crohn's, or indeed if you have Celiac.

For the Crohn's patient it is best that the pure spearmint leaf is chewed;
> and then spit out once you have inhaled all the oils from it,
> once your tongue tingles from the leaf.

191 Crohn's disease requires a release of tension first and foremost.
It requires the release of all wheat products,
> of any type of wheat products.

It requires, in terms of flours, only the ingestion of oat flour.
It also requires not of any citrus for a period of three months.
For the first three months
> the alkaline must take precedence over the acidic.

And then, after three months the balance may be maintained,
> equal on both.

No caffeine for three months, no alcohol for three months.
During the three months, no peppers of any sort.
Also, during the three months,
> the being will ingest as much as possible, uncooked vegetables.

This is in order to gain from the vegetables all the nutrients that is possible.
The being will also, during the three month period,
> refrain from an excessive use of salt;
> no more than one teaspoon per day,
> whether in the food that is cooked, or in the raw food.

We would also recommend that during the three month period,
> the daily exercise of ten minutes of vigorous walking twice daily.

And by vigorous, Soul, we mean the arms pumping,
> the legs pumping almost within a march cadence.

During the three month period, no milk products of any kind.
This regimen will assist the Soul to heal.
We would also suggest that a habit be entertained for eating,
> and that daily one leaf of pure peppermint is ingested,
> not just underneath the tongue, but actually swallowed.

This may be place within your salad, or within your bun,
> but not cooked beforehand, Soul, it is to be placed raw, as is.

We would also recommend the use of oregano,
> preferably fresh, but alternatively dried,
> using one teaspoon dried, to half teaspoon fresh.

And we would recommend that this be used as often as possible
> within the cooking, within any sauce, within any salad,
> within any dressing oregano will add a healthy aspect to the meal.

It is akin to the pure peppermint.

192 We would speak on the properties of the
> the deep golden orange or the white lily.

The others indeed have properties, but are not nearly as efficacious
> and so we will limit it to those two colors.

The insides of the lily, that pollen that often you brush against,
> this may be collected, placed within water;
> one half teaspoon pollen to one quart water.

The water is to be set in glass container,
> set out in the sun for three hours.

You may then shake to make sure it is well blended.

Ingested daily this will assist those with Crohn's disease
    or any like manner of intestinal problems.
The first day one tablespoon,
    the second day two tablespoon six hours apart,
    the third day one tablespoon six hours apart.
This will soothe the being and stimulate the body's healing capacity,
    the mechanism of healing.
It will also be of assistance for those beings who suffer from heartburn,
    whether it is caused by your reflux, or by irritation to your inners.
In those cases one teaspoon will be sufficient, once daily.

193 The inner workings of the evening primrose flower bud
    are most efficacious in cases of extreme distress,
    distension of the abdomen.
This is particularly helpful to those who have diarrhea,
    to those who have been unable to stop the diarrhea
    by any other method.
In that particular case, Souls of earth,
    you will be required to ingest five of these.
It may be either in the fresh state or in the dried state.
For if it is dried in the manner which we shall give,
    it will retain the majority of its efficacity.
To dry, you will take the evening primrose bud when it has just opened,
    and remove the flower petals,
    place the actual bud inners where it may dry.
And it is to be left there, uncovered for three days.
On the third day you may then place a covering over it
    until it becomes desiccated,
    and we would suggest that the covering not be manmade.
Once it has become desiccated,
    and that will depend upon the humidity
    within your particular portion of earth,
    you may then place within a tightly covered jar
    and store in a cool dried area.
It will retain its efficacity for up to two years.
In all cases, it is most efficacious if there have been
    no additional pesticides or chemicals used.

194 For those who have ulcerative colitis,
    the daily ingestion of one drop of oil of pure peppermint
    will assist the being.

195 We would bring you to the study of the cornflower.
It provides soothing relief to the internal digestive system,
    especially in cases of ulcerated esophagus
    and ulcerated stomach linings.
It would even, Souls, comfort the ulcerated colitis.
We would have you take upon first bloom of the cornflower
    ten petals, only the petals.
They are to be placed in a small container of purified water.
Only small amount so that the petals float lightly on top.
The container of the water must be of glass
    or the palms if glass is not available.
You may then ingest the water and the petals,
    ten petals each time until the pain recedes.
This may be done each hour.
The water, Souls, is for ease of the passage of the petals down the throat
    for if you were to chew them any length of time,
    there would be a bitterness and there would be a lessening
    of the facility that enters in your being.
The efficaciousness is in the whole petal entering in
    and mingling with the juices, the acidic juices of the body.
It sets up a chemical reaction that soothes the excess acid,
    that soothes the burning sensation.
This may also be used for children but we would advise that
    in the case of a young child, no more than five petals
    are to be ingested within each two hour period,
    and no more than three periods in a day.
And because the young child may have difficulty swallowing,
    a concoction of honey and water may be brought together
    and given to the child.

196 We would, Soul, caution that all information
    is to be utilized from the flower, from the plant
    that is without taint of pesticide, herbicide, or growth hormones.
All of those chemicals will prevent the efficacy of the remedy.
The rose petals are to be plucked when the dew touches the petals.
Cutting the petals interferes with the potency of the remedy.
You will use the yellow petals.
Place in water covering the petals, in the sun for two hours.
This will enable the properties to enter in to the water.
The water must not be hot or refrigerated.
Tepid will be fine.

The yellow rose petals and the resultant remedious waters
> are helpful for the gastritis, internal upsets.
>> Irritation of the stomach area and those organs within the area
>> will be remedied by the ingestion of these waters.

A teaspoon full each hour for six hours
> each day until the problem is resolved.

197 We would speak upon the properties of the dandelion.
You already know many uses for the dandelion.
We would particularly bring your attention
> to the inner center of the dandelion,
> after the leaves have been removed.

There is a round core.
And they are to be ingested at the rate of one every six hours
> until the pain has receded.

This is most efficacious, internally swallowed,
> for those who have gastritis or any disease of the colon area.

That does not include cancer, Soul.
It is efficacious also for the young child who is afflicted with the colic.
In this case it would be one quarter of an average sized bud.
Remember to remove the petals.

198 The sprig of parsley is a beneficial plant.
We speak of the parsley raised
> to know no pesticide, to know no contact with toxic endeavours.

The parsley leaf, the frilly leaf, is of benefit to the ailments of the intestine.
It is in its state of freshness of beneficial efficacy to irritated bowels.
Dry the fresh until crumbly.
In crumbled state, mash fine, and place sparingly upon food.
Do not cook in any form.
Do not boil, do not fry, do not put in hot food.
For intestinal disorders only, a sprinkle upon the food before ingestion,
> three times daily, until irritation is eased.

199 For the adult who has cramps within the digestion,
> we would have you develop an infusion
> comprised of three parts water to one part pure spearmint,
> so that if you have three tablespoons of water
> you will have one tablespoon pure spearmint leaves.

Then, Soul, you will place pure spearmint within the water
    and let sit for a period of no more than six hours.
This may be taken orally by mouth,
    one teaspoon of the leaves that have been soaked in the water,
    to be mashed within the teeth.
You will chew them and allow the oil to enter in
    and down into your stomach, and it will ease the cramps.

200 For dysentery, diarrhea, we would speak upon
    the properties of the dahlia bulb.
Each plant upon the earth has been placed
    for a particular and very specific reason.
In each area of the earth you will find there are plants of healing
    even in your arid deserts.
And that is why, Souls of earth,
    one of the reasons for dried portions of a healing plant;
    for in the arid desert, they are not prevalent;
    for in floods, they are not available;
    for in the ice packed areas of your earth,
    they are only available at a certain time.
And hence the Creator planned the dried efficacity of many plants.
The dahlia bulb requires you to remove the outer covering
    that protects the bulb and to reach within,
        only one thirty second of an inch, a small shaving no more
        than one inch in length and one eighth inch in width.
This will be enough for three applications of the remedy.
This minute portion is to be dried until it has withered
    and then you may store it until you require its usage.
When it is needed, Souls, you will place the withered portion
    that has been stored in glass container
    within a minute amount of water.
It will be ready for infusion
    when it has plumped up and absorbed the water.
The water which has been purified need only cover the sliver.
As the sliver plumps up with the water, it releases within the water
    its efficacity.
One teaspoon from one sliver
    is all that is necessary to soothe the colicky baby,
    to soothe the pain, the cramps from the diarrhea.

It matters not whether the child is one day old
    or it is an older, of eighty years old,
    one teaspoon is the dosage for all.
At any point in time when dysentery attacks the being or malaria,
    one teaspoon is to be given each hour until the symptoms abate.
You may, Souls of earth, pass on slivers to those who have no way
    or do not have the climate to raise these bulbs.
Indeed, we suggest the drying of many pieces for future use.

201   We would have you make a paste using honey and clover.
The clover will include the bud and two leaves of each plant
    that you remove the bud from.
Gather twelve buds, twenty four leaves,
    and while they are still in their fresh state
        mix them with one quarter cup honey, until they are blended.
Then place two drops rosemary oil
    and again stir until it is fully blended.
This concoction is most efficacious for the external assistance
    of dysentery.
On the left quadrant, you would place between the navel
    and just below the rib.
You will find an indent, a natural indent just below the rib
    and you will place this paste in a circular motion.
The diameter will be approximately three inches to four inches.
And you will allow that to stay.
When it dries, you will then proceed to do the same
    with the right hand side.
You will find this of great assistance
    to calming the inners, to stopping the explosions.
We would request that you not wipe this off
    until you are ready for another application.
Each application to be done four hours apart until you are calm inside.

202   The pine cone has within it capability to cease the diarrhea.
It is found in the core, not in the outer leaves.
Within the core, you will find a kernel and that kernel, ground, mashed,
    mixed with water and a dollop of honey, will cease diarrhea.
The proportion is one eighth teaspoon of the kernel,
    one half teaspoon of the honey
        to be ingested by those at age five and above.

For five and below, we would suggest the honey be halved
> so that in cases of severe diarrhea it may enter the system quickly.

This will be necessary in cases of emergency treatment
> that has been long denied and the patient is dehydrated.

203 We will speak on the bright yellow marigold.
You will find the marigold powder is efficacious
> in the treatment of the diaper rash.

Take the petals,
> only the petals, and carefully dry them,
>> then grind them into a powder.

Placed liberally upon the rash,
> it prevents a further moisture from exacerbating the rash.

204 We would discuss the flower of this star anise plant.
There will be petals, there will be seeds.
We will take first the petals.
The petals are to be used in their moist state.
Drying of the petals provides no efficacy.
One half of a petal of the star anise
> may be used to increase the digestive aid
> for those who suffer from a celiac disease,
> those who have the ulcer within the duodenum,
> those who have difficulty with absorption of calcium
> and other vitamins.

You may ingest safely the same amount each day
> until you feel an improvement within your being.

And then, Soul,
> you will restrain the ingestion of half the petal to every other day.

Over a period of fourteen days, all will notice improvement.
You will then gradually decrease the number of times you ingest.
From every other day, it will then be once weekly
> and then only once every thirty days
>> for maintenance of healthy flora within the system.

205 We would speak on the properties of the cabbage family;
> specifically cabbage, in itself,
>> the red cabbage and the cauliflower.

Both have interchangeable qualities
> and so whatever is to hand will be sufficient.

The outer leaves of the cabbage, not the inner,
> may be used as an enhancement to the healing of the ulcer.

They are not to be taken internally for the healing.
They are to be made into a poultice
> and placed externally upon the point of the ulcer.

Whether it is of the esophagus or gastro.
You will take no less than ten leaves, warmed in olive oil,
> not hot, two degrees above room temperature would be ideal.

Then it is to be placed within a coarse fabric such as what you call towel,
> and placed upon the point of ulcer for one half hour.

This will provide soothing and will eventually heal the ulcer
> provided the original cause of the ulcer is no longer present.

And so, Souls, if the ulcer was caused by stress
> and stress is no longer present, then the healing may take place.

But if the original cause is maintained, then you will continue
> to experience the ulcer.

In either case, the poultice will provide relief
> but can not provide long term healing
> > unless the original cause has been terminated.

206 For the being who has difficulty with the bowels,
> constipation is that of which we speak.

Daily three leaves pure spearmint at least three centimeters long.
This will bring balance to the daily elimination of the bowel.

207 Souls of earth, we come unto you
> to speak upon the subject of constipation,
> > for it becomes a very serious problem for your aged.

And it becomes in many cases life threatening to their being.
In all manner of cases the most efficacious methodology is of course
> an intake of dark green leafy vegetables,
> > three cups per day as a preventative that is raw where possible.

If it is cooked then it should be doubled to six cups per day.
This is for those who have difficulty.
Not for those who have no difficulty with the constipation.
For the child we would recommend only one and a half cups
> from the ages of two to twelve daily.

It may, when cooked, be two cups.
It may be pureed for those who have difficulty swallowing or chewing.
And this will not affect its efficacity.

We especially recommend the chard, the kale and the spinach.
To be effective it must be daily ingested.
There will come a time, Souls of earth,
> when you will not have available your concoctions
>> that you ingest now to overcome the constipation.

And this remedy will alleviate the pain
> associated with the severe or even moderate constipation.

We would also suggest the intake of liquid such as water.
For the young child ages two to twelve, three cups per day minimum.
For the older, beyond twelve, we would suggest five cups per day.
We say liquid such as water, for weak tea may also help.
That weak tea, we would suggest,
> only the pure peppermint and the chamomile.

Your greens or blacks will not assist.
A teaspoon of burdock may be placed within the weak tea,
> one teaspoon for every three cups.

208 We would speak on the efficacy of the plumeria.
The plumeria holds a remedy
> for the constipation of the intestinal tract.

The remedy resides within the stamen of the plant.
It is simply the snipping off of stamen,
> rubbing it between the fingers
> or you may grind it with your mortar and pestle.

You will require no more than one quarter teaspoon of the ground powder.
This may be ingested in water or juice.
You may even mix it in with a cool tea.
It is especially efficacious when mixed in with a cool green tea.
If there is no movement within a two hour period,
> then an ingestion of another one quarter teaspoon is prescribed.

This may be given every two hours until the movement occurs.
It is a gentle form of laxative and may be given even to children
> as young as five years.

209 An incipient infection in the bladder.
We would suggest, Soul, that you cut back on all salt intake for three days,
> that you increase water intake by three glasses
> for three days and that you ingest cranberry.

This may be in capsule or pill
> or as three eight ounce glasses unsweetened cranberry juice.

It must be unsweetened, for sweetened will defeat the purpose.
When it is capsule or pill derived from pure cranberry juice,
    a total of fifteen hundred milligrams per day for three days.
You will then ingest two capsules or pills of five hundred
    or one eight ounce unsweetened cranberry juice for three more days
    and on the seventh day you will need only one capsule or pill
    or four ounces unsweetened cranberry juice for the next ten days.

210   We would discuss with you pressure points.
Turning the hands over with the thumb and the forefinger pressed together,
    and entwining the three fingers,
        the right into the left, the left on the outside.
And then placing your hands in this position
    toward your being, will assist in the healing
    of a minor bladder infection.
Place your hands in front of the navel area.
Ten times separate the thumb and the forefinger
    and bring them back together.
A deep breath and you have completed.

211   We would have you institute a kidney flush.
You will, Soul, ingest cranberry[21],
    without aluminum or sugar, twice daily, three days.
Drink copious amounts of water and fruit juice, unsweetened.
Those juices that are acidic are to be ingested
    but no more than three eight ounce glasses per day.
You must, Soul, refrain from the ingestion of protein during the three days
    and ensure as much as possible,
        the cleansing of all food intake of toxin.
And we would suggest the intake of pure peppermint tea;
    ingest three cups per day during the three days.

212   Flowers are useful in the healing of parasites
    within the human body.
Pinworms within the beings may be chased out by the ingestion
    of a minute portion of the leaf of the gardenia.

---

21 cranberry - 1000 milligrams powder or two eight ounce glasses unsweetened cranberry juice.

Ensure that no ingestion takes place with the bud of the gardenia,
> or with the leaf when it is in bud.

The plant must be in full, and we stress full bloom for efficacy
> of the process of chasing out the worm.

Soul, ensure no gardenia toxicity by full growth and cleanse pesticide
> by salt water soak five minutes before use[22].

For the baby, for the little one who can not chew,
> for the old one who can not chew,
> for those who have lost the ability to chew;
> mash, make paste of the leaf, grind it into minute particles
> so that ingestion is possible for these Souls.

213 We would bring to you a remedy
> for those afflicted with diseases of the liver.

We would have you understand, Souls of earth,
> there are many complications involved
> in the destruction of a fully operating liver.

All manners of toxicity and excesses will affect the operating of the liver.

It is a finely balanced, a finely tuned organ and can be overwhelmed,
> to the point where it almost ceases operation
> and in many cases people will pass because it has ceased operation.

Liver diseases such as cirrhosis may be brought out
> by excessive toxins within, by tainted blood, by tainted air.

Recall the toxins in the air enter in to the skin
> and over time, when one is exposed to great toxicities
> or ingests great toxicities, the liver becomes overwhelmed,
> becomes hardened and can not filter.

And so we offer unto you a remedy to cleanse the liver
> and assist it in operating at its peak level.

For those who have already knowledge of severe cirrhosis of your liver,
> we would suggest that you carry out the remedy
> thrice within a three month period of time.

For those who have no knowledge of cirrhosis of the liver
> but know they have been ingesting excessive amounts of toxicity
> in whatever manner, we would suggest once every six months.

During a ten day period there will be no ingestion of flesh,
> only vegetables, nuts, legumes.

---

22 salt water - to one fourth cup water, add one teaspoon salt.
After the five minutes rinse thoroughly before use.

During those ten days liquid is important.
One eight ounce glass purified water must be ingested every two hours,
    up unto ten glasses per day as maximum.
Each day for three of the glasses, you will rinse within the water
    one drop rosemary oil.
It may be three in a row or every other, but it is to be done three times.
You will also place on your food, not cooked,
    one half teaspoon rosemary twice daily.
Three times daily you will place one half teaspoon ground star anise.
This may be folded into your food
    and cooked every day of the ten days.
You will also for those ten days,
    preferably ingest no tobacco and no caffeine,
    no drugs that are toxic to your system.
We understand, Souls of earth,
    that you may be on a prescribed medication and we do not deny this
    nor do we suggest that you leave your prescribed medication.
But those drugs that are addictive,
    we ask that you refrain from for the ten day period.
Each day during the ten day period,
    five minutes of exercise each hour is necessary.
This is to be done every hour for eight hours.
The exercise whether sitting in a chair or walking,
    must involve some vigorous activity
    whether it is the waving of the arms or the waving of the feet
    or a vigorous massage for those who are unable to move.
The blood, the cells of your body must be invigorated,
    must provide that extra energy to your floundering liver.
At the end of the ten days we would suggest
    that you follow the remedy
    to the extent that you only gradually reintroduce into your being
    the flesh, the caffeine or tobacco.
This is for those Souls who have excessive toxins within their being,
    we would bring unto you a color during the remedy for your liver,
    and that is an oxblood color.
Lay a cloth of that color across your abdomen,
    or wear for ten days ribbons of that color
    around the wrist and the ankle.
The vibration of that color enters in and assists
    in the reconstruction of the process of your liver.

The cloth, if laid upon your abdomen, should be laid
> once every hour for the eight hours.

If it is a color that you bring into your being with the eye,
> that too is to be done once every hour.

In either case, three minutes will suffice.
The ribbons you may leave on for the three minutes
> or you may leave on during the whole day or evening.

The vibration of that color reminds the body
> of its optimum healing potential and so assists in reconstructing.

Before retiring for your daily sleep during this ten day process
> you will place upon the bottom of each foot one drop of rosemary.

It is to be within the center of the sole of the foot.
Simply place and massage in one drop.
Souls of earth, the liver is the workhorse of thy being.
It is that which takes the brunt of what you do to your being.
It is that which must cleanse the toxins that you ingest into thy being.
There is only so much toxins that it can freely deliver
> and cleanse before it becomes overwhelmed.

Souls we would teach you, do not overburden thy being.

214 The plant, star anise, will progress to healing
> of an ailment within the liver.

You may use a quarter teaspoon of ground leaf of star anise daily
> for a period of thirteen days to effect a cure of any liver disease.

This dosage is only for those who are above the age of thirteen
> and in stable health.

For the very, very frail, and for those under the age of thirteen
> it is recommended for one eighth of a teaspoon
> for the same period of time.

It would be detrimental to increase the dosage for the frail and the young.
It would defeat the purpose of the healing
> and we strongly advise against an overdose.

215 The periwinkle, Souls of earth, is most efficacious
> when ground to a fine pulp.

You would use the leaves in this particular instance.
The leaves are to be dried, sun dried, and then ground to a fine powder.
The powder is then mixed with purified water
> in the ratio of one teaspoon of the powder to two cups water.

In the cases of cancer of the stomach or the bowel,
> the ingestion will be one teaspoon per day.

In cases where the cancer has rapidly advanced,
> you may safely ingest up to half a teaspoon every hour for five hours,
>> only for the first two days
>> and thereafter revert back to the original dosage.

The flowers of the periwinkle are not for ingestion.
It is not, Soul, that they will poison your being.
It is that they would provide an imbalance within your being
> and so we do not recommend the flowers, only the leaves.

216 You need only strip a thin slice of the bark of the juniper.
The bark is to be dried and then ground into a fine powder.
This powder may then be mixed with olive oil
> and placed upon the genital area
> for any one afflicted with the genital warts or eruptions,
> rashes, any irritation.

It is to be placed on the outside,
> not the inside of the genital area for the female, near the labia.

Legs

217 In those cases where the patient is confined to a wheelchair
> and has difficulty with the knees, any sort of difficulty,
> the slight massage of each knee daily with the olive oil
> and once weekly using of the oil of bergamot,
> one drop to one tablespoon olive oil as a lubricant upon the knee.

218 For those confined to wheelchair
> who experience pains within the thigh area,
> we would recommend once weekly massage gently
> with two drops eucalyptus oil to half cup olive oil.

The massage is not to be the whole thigh.
It will be sufficient to do only a strip along the top of the thigh
> and a strip in the middle along the back of the thigh.

This will help provide ease from those pains.
For those who experience pains
> in the lower legs that are confined to wheelchairs,
> we would recommend the application of the olive oil remedy[23].

This may be done daily.

---

23 olive oil remedy - in one quarter cup olive oil will be placed three drops oil of lavender, one drop oil of rosemary, one drop oil of geranium.

219 For the leg stretch in a chair:
   without using your hands, pull your toes towards your being,
   and as you feel your leg and the thigh stretch, slowly release.
And do the same with the opposite leg.
And you have thereby stretched your whole body
   and your mind in a matter of moments.

220 Shin splints.
We would have the being place upon both shins,
   in fact the whole leg from the knee to the ankle,
   a mix of lavender and olive oil.
To one quarter cup of olive oil, three drops lavender oil.
It is not required to use the full quarter cup each time.
Place this upon legs in the evening before the rest for the night.
Rub it into the legs, Soul.
Do not wash them until the morning.
Use lightly not copious.
We would also ask that in the morning, upon arising, and before the wash,
   stand against a wall, the back to the wall.
And then places feet pigeon toed, so that the large toes of each foot touch,
   and then pull them apart and spread them the opposite way out.
And then together again, and then out, and then together again, and out,
   three times.
Do not lift off the floor.
It is to be done flat on the floor.
It is particular to individual beings.
Some may require fourteen days, some may require less.
The remedy of the olive oil and lavender has many uses
   to penetrate the muscles of the being, to stimulate healing of bone,
   but in various capacities depending upon the pain.

221 You will understand the ache that is felt within the legs
   may be ameliorated by the use of olive oil with a touch of ginger oil,
   one quarter cup olive oil, one drop ginger oil.
If there is no ginger oil available, shave finely and dice finely
   half a teaspoon ginger mixed with the olive oil
   and rub onto the legs at night before retiring with sleep.

222 To relieve stress and strain,
   even to relieve the varicose veins,

place the lighter shades of purple, the violet, the lavender
upon the backs of the legs until the pain decreases.

223 There are varying degrees of the syndrome called restless leg.
In the initial stages of the syndrome
it would prove efficacious to the patient to be bathed in a salt water.
Those who do not have access to the salt water,
may in their homes stimulate the tap water,
the well water with the sea salt.
A minute measurement is all that is required.
One tablespoon for each inch of water.
Soul, the water will be room temperature.
Cold water would shock the system.
Even in the most sun burning of climates,
understand it will shock the venous system,
the veins within the legs
and on up into the hips and down through the toes.
There is to be a vigorous rubbing of the legs, feet and toes
before the immersion in the room temperature salt water.
If immersion is not possible,
cloths soaked in the salt water
may be applied to the torso of the body.
When total immersion is not possible,
you will start with the cloths above the belly button.
When the cloth is applied, it is done and left upon the body
until the cloth ceases to retain the salt.
Once the salt has been absorbed by the flesh,
the cloths are removed and the body is rinsed.
For those that have immersed themselves totally,
it is important that they are rinsed off before they dry the body.
And the same will be done for the patient with the cloths.
You will take clean cloth and gently swab the body.
Do not attempt to force the salt crystals in the flesh.
We would have you understand stress in all its forms
aggravates all illnesses, without exception, all illnesses of earth.

224 Deeper into the color of green so that it is beyond the pales
and yet not full into the spectrum of green,
this color is efficacious for those who have tremors of the leg,
called restless leg syndrome.
A covering of this shade will ease.

225 You will understand, Soul, that the darker blue pansies
   are most efficacious for breaks of the knees,
      of the lower leg, of the feet.
Take five of the whole flowers, and grind them until they separate.
Once they have separated, place over them
      one tablespoon of water along with one eighth teaspoon of salt.
It may be sea salt or ground salt.
Let that sit for a period of forty five minutes.
And then grind again until you have a paste.
Do not be concerned about the salt.
Leave it as is.
If it is not fully dissolved, that is acceptable.
Once you have ground this into a paste,
   you will place that paste directly upon the broken area.
And hold it pressing the broken area very lightly
      for a minimum of twelve minutes.
You may, Soul, place bandage to hold it in place
      or you may simply hold it in your hand.
This will reduce the swelling and stimulate the healing of the broken area.

226 We speak to you of hip problems,
   whether they are rheumatic, arthritic,
   whether they are birth defect,
      the misalignment of the disks as often occurs in a birth,
   or brought about by lack of nutrition
      where the bones become brittle.
Also there are the ligaments and muscles that come into play with hip problems.
The nutrition is important from a young age but it may also
      be improved upon as an adult where food is not a scarcity.
If you have access to an abundance of foods,
   we highly recommend dark green leafy vegetables;
   a minimum one and a half cups each day
      to improve the strength of the bone,
      to enhance the tone of the muscle.
If you begin as a child, we would suggest half a cup daily
      as soon as the child is old enough to chew on its own.
This will ensure stability of the bone and the muscle.
We would also have you understand the effect that beta carotene has
      upon the wellness of bone density.

And that from the time of childhood one half carrot per day
> will assist in the strength of the bone and the density.

As an adult, if there has been lack of carrot in childhood,
> two carrots per day to maintain and to enhance the bone density.

227 To those who are afflicted with the hip problem,
> whether it be arthritic or rheumatoidic,
> we would suggest particular attention be paid
> to the inner portion of the sole of the foot, the arch area,
> the whole arch area, but particularly on the inner edge.

This is to be massaged gently
> with a mixture of pure peppermint oil and olive oil,
> > one quarter cup olive oil and two drops pure peppermint
> in this case.

And that same mixture remedy is to be placed
> upon the outer edges of the hips.

Again, Soul, in a gentle circular massage.

It is not necessary to cover the whole hip.

It is the outer edges that are most sensitive to the application.

228 You will find upon your earth, many who practice full running,
> to have a variety of injuries to their being.

Many are more prone to arthritics.

Many are more prone to damaging the bones.

We would have you understand, if you have a necessity to run full tilt daily,
> to use the application of a mixture of one half cup olive oil,
> > one drop geranium oil, one drop rosemary and one drop lavender
> upon your legs up to your top of your thighs including your feet

This will help to obviate some of the stressors placed upon your being.

Feet

229 The tansy may be placed within the shoe
> near the sole of your foot to absorb bacteria,
> > especially in places of the countries that are toxic,
> > especially in places where excrement is not always cleansed.

This is, Soul, a preventative.

Three leaves placed within each shoe or sole of a sandal will be efficacious.

230 Souls of earth, we would recommend
> the daily application of the olive oil onto the feet.

A small amount will do.

231   The leaves of the pansy may be used to cleanse the feet.
For those who have difficulties with the athlete's feet,
>with the carbuncles upon the feet,
>>it would be most efficacious to use the leaves
>>within a concoction of olive oil.

Place the leaves within the olive oil as is;
>fresh leaves, two per foot,
>dried leaves four per foot.

And then slather on the leaves and the olive oil
>and allow it to sit for one half hour.

And then, Soul, you may brush off the leaves.

232   The dandelion is efficacious for what you call athlete's foot,
>that fungus that attacks the feet.

Take the petals of at least four dandelions,
>crunch them within your palm, grind them within your palm.

What you have done with your palm is heat the petals,
>so that it is easier to grind them and to release the fungi fighting.

You will then place four drops olive oil and again grind
>until you have almost a liquid of the petals
>and then place that in between each toe and underneath the toes.

It matters not if it is only on one area, all of them must be done.
And you will hold the concoction between the toes and under the toes
>for at least fifteen minutes.

Repeat this thrice each day until you are healed.
You will find, Soul, much relief from the itching and burning.

233   You have upon your earth the droppings from your cedars.
You may take a half cup of these fallen brown needles,
>place them in boiling water.

Steep for five minutes minimum,
>strain and allow the strained water to cool[24].

Full strength, Soul, that which you have strained is most efficacious
>for what you call your fungus of the foot.

Soaked within a compress or directly placing the foot in the water
>for a period of five minutes each time
>will eliminate the fungus from the foot.

Those who have fungus even upon the nails of the hands
>and upon the secreted places of the body where moisture collects

---

24   cool - bring the boiled water slowly to room temperature.

may also use a wash with this water
to inhibit the growth of the fungus.

234 At the first bloom of the purple iris
pluck the whole head of the flower.
Hold it in your hand and rub until it becomes a gooey mass.
Allow it to dry along with other heads of the iris,
until you have a half cup of dried iris heads.
That half cup is most efficacious
when placed in water that will cover the feet.
The water need not be warmed, and it should not be icy cold either.
Room temperature, Soul.
All feet that have been troubled with itching,
whether it be due to diabetes or due to a fungus,
this will ease the itching.
Simply rest your feet within this concoction for fifteen minutes each day
until the condition has passed.

235 To remove fungus, a rash, carbuncle from the area of your feet,
you must, Souls, also address your digestion.
For to address only one will be placing a short term bandaid.
When you have a problem with your feet in this regard,
you will need to remove from your diet all peppers
for a period of four days.
You will also for the four day period
remove from your diet wheat and cabbage.
And you will see a great improvement,
a healing of the rash or the fungus, the carbuncle.

236 For those Souls of earth who are afflicted with foot diseases
that cause open sores and itching or burning,
we would suggest mixing within a one quarter cup of olive oil,
half a teaspoon of honey mixed thoroughly,
and apply to all of the affected areas.
Do not wash away for at least a three hour period
so that the skin will absorb the healing properties.
The reason for the olive oil is that it gives an added healing,
also it is easier to place upon the skin and is soothing to the open sore.
And it allows, it is as a carrier for the properties of the honey to enter in.

This is also the case for large burned areas of the body
> where it is not just a short, small burn.

In larger burns mixing with the olive oil
> allows the carrier to enter in to the open sores.

237 We would give you remedy for tired aching feet, burning feet.
Take one half teaspoon ground rosemary,
> mixed with one tablespoon olive oil and one drop lavender.

Rub this mixture upon the palms of your hands.
And then proceed to rub it upon your feet,
> starting with the top of your feet and then the soles.

Allow the mixture to sit for at least a minimum six minutes.
It will provide ease.
It will stop the burning.
It will stop the ache.
At the end of the six minutes
> you may proceed to use a cloth dipped in olive oil
> and gently remove the rosemary from the feet.

Washing will inhibit the benefits.
It is enough to use the olive oil to remove the rest of the rosemary.
It is the ground rosemary that will be most efficacious.

238 For the feet, mix a concoction of two drops of lavender oil,
> to one quarter cup of olive oil,
>> with the addition of two drops of pure peppermint oil.

Massaged into the feet,
> it will soothe the soreness, it will soothe the heat.

Massage gently in a circular motion,
> take the toes of each foot and gently
>> after you have placed the concoction, pull each three times,
>> starting from the large toe going to the small toe.

You will than take the index finger and place it beneath the toes
> and firmly bring it down
>> from the large toe to the small toe, three times.

And as a final, from the two toes next to the big toe,
> draw down with the index finger the whole length of the foot.

239 For those who have the burning feet,

oil of pure peppermint, one drop in a quarter cup of olive oil,
and then smoothed upon the bottom of the feet nightly,
> will grant them ease of sleep,
> will grant them ease from the pain of the burning.

240 The feet require attention when they are burning,
> when they are becoming numb.

This occurs in various diseases.
And their linking unto the shoulder area
> is applicable to burning or numb feet.

In those cases you will receive comfort
> from the placing of a dab of lavender oil
> down the center of the sole of the foot
> and a corresponding dab across the top of the shoulders
> and you will feel an easing.

241 We would have you understand the color purple
> abounds upon your earth
> in plants, trees, indeed even crystals.

You have within nature many examples of this color
> in all varying shades.

For feet that are in pain, feet that are overworked,
> feet that are tired and strained,
> when you know you will be standing and walking
> for great distances, place five leaves or petals[25]
> within that with which your feet are shod.

It will alleviate and allow you greater capacity to stand or walk.

242 Pure peppermint is efficacious for tired and aching feet,
> feet that have walked long distances whether shod or unshod.

Make the tea as directed or use the tincture as directed
> and merely swab the soles of the feet.

This is also most efficacious for those beings who have burning feet
> due to circulatory problems or Parkinson or restless leg syndrome.

If you are using fresh pure peppermint leaves,
> then you need only four large leaves
> to be brewed for the three minutes,
> within the one and a half cups water.

---

25 five leaves or petals – use the Lavender or Violet plant.

The tea is to be boiled for three minutes.
If you are using leaves you will use
> one tablespoon to one and a half cups water,
> and steeping only for three minutes.

And then you may strain and use.

243 We would speak with you on the properties on the blackberry.
It has long been known to have efficacious effects upon the skin.
Blackberry tea is most efficacious for tired aching feet.
It is not the ripe blackberries we speak of, it is the green,
> that is where the properties are most efficacious
> for application to the body.

For one cup of tea take six of the green berries,
> steep in hot water five minutes.

It does not have to be boiling.
Strain the berries and then apply the cooled tea
> to the soles of the feet and the tops of the
> feet and allow to air dry.

This may be done four to five times per day
> depending upon the severity of the pain.

You may even, Souls of earth, soak the feet within this tea.
You may for future use rinse the little green berries
> and dry them out of the sun upon a natural surface
> until they become shriveled.

Once they are rinsed, you must dry them thoroughly.
Once they are shriveled grind them into a powder.
You will need only one eighth of a teaspoon
> of this powder per one cup of water.

Mix the powder
> once the water has been heated to just before boiling.

And then, allow it to sit for five minutes before cooling and using.

244 The rosemary needles, when placed in warm water,
> not hot, Souls, warm water, with a drop of lavender
> and a drop of geranium and enough water to cover the feet,
> will provide relaxation.

For those beings who have had to be on their feet all day for their work,
> the rosemary needles must be at least twelve within the water.

And you will allow them to sit in the water for five minutes
> before plunging your feet into the mixture.

You may then sit until the water cools.

245 We would offer remedies for those beings afflicted with bunions.
Make a paste of one tablespoon baking soda,
    one eighth teaspoon olive oil and one eighth teaspoon honey.
Mix and apply the paste to the bunion
    every four hours of waking time for three days.
The bunion will soften.
After you feel it soften,
    you will then place the application only twice daily.
The application must be left on for at least twelve minutes,
    and no more than fifteen minutes each time.
Continue with the daily application until
    the hardness and the soreness have receded.

246 The white onion sliced vertically is efficacious
    for feet that are dried and cracked.
Place the feet in a bowl of warm water and
    allow one half of the onion
        to rest within the water for fifteen seconds,
        and then take the onion while in the water
        and rub it around the affected area.

Full Body

Skin
247 Souls of earth, we would have you understand
how sensitive the skin of your body is
to all manner of temperature,
to all manner of moisture, to all manner of dust,
to all matter period.
Your skin is a sense mechanism and it is a process mechanism.
For your skin processes all that comes in contact with it.
It absorbs all that come in contact with it.
It is as a sensor.
It is as a sponge.
It is as a computer.
What goes in is processed.
It is not merely a covering.
It is so much more.
It requires, Souls of earth, care.
It is no less important what goes on your skin, what enters in to your skin
than what enters in to the body.
When you enter in to pollution it is the skin that is absorbing it.
Not just the breath, not just the lungs, the nostrils, indeed not.
All exposed areas of the skin also absorb.
For when it is absorbed by the skin, it is then into the cellular layer.
Daily, we would suggest the placing of olive oil
upon the extremities of your being, the hands and the feet,
so that that goodness is absorbed within the being
and sends messages of positive into your cells.
Place within one quarter cup olive oil, two drops vanilla,
this will enhance the efficacy of the olive oil,
when a being is recuperating from a severe trauma.

We would suggest the whole body,
>   once every three days, be massaged lightly.

This will enhance the healing capability of the body.
And any particular area that is being attacked by disease
>   may also be lightly massaged.

248   Souls, we speak on the barberry leaves,
>   the root and the berries themselves.

We would have you know this plant is efficacious
>   for those who have the disease of the muscles.

It is not only the dystrophy but the tremors caused by the Parkinson's.
The muscles become as infected with toxins.
There is a toxicity that settles within the bend of the muscles.
You will understand the application of the barberry leaves is external.
The leaves are not to be crushed.
They are to be warmed.
Cover eight leaves in purified water,
>   and bring the water to room temperature.

This will allow the healing properties to begin releasing.
The body will be washed with this water.
You need not soak the body.
A wiping is sufficient, but do not dry the body with a cloth.
You will allow the air to dry.
Take the leaves from the water and place upon the areas most in need.
Do so with a light covering that will hold the leaves in place
>   for a minimum of twenty three minutes.

The root of the barberry, and we do not advocate digging up the plant
>   and killing it, merely borrowing from the plant a bit of its root,
>   a quarter of an inch of your earth measurement is sufficient.

This root is to be dried in the sun and then ground into fine grains.
The grains may be placed underneath the tongue once daily.
It requires only a dab.
Minuscule, Souls, not a teaspoon, not one thirty second of a teaspoon.
Simply a small dab.
This will be done for those with the Parkinson until the tremors ease
>   and then a weekly maintenance of the dab will suffice.

A small handful of the berries may be boiled as a tea would be boiled.
They are to be steeped for five minutes.
This may be used as a tonic,
>   a minute amount, a sip is all that is required.

Let it sit underneath the tongue and dissolve.
This application will assist internally
> in cleansing the muscles of their toxicity.
You may sip throughout the day.

249   We would speak on the uses of the sweet potato[26].
The sweet potato has high quantity of natural sugars within.
This may be utilized in various concoctions to assist
> in the healing of those ailments that affect the flesh,
> be they psoriasis, be they eczema, be they allergic reaction,
> be they a reaction of scabies, of hives.
To soothe the skin when any of these have erupted,
> you will take a cooked sweet potato and mash it finely.
Place one half cup of the mashed fine sweet potato in a cloth sieve.
Lift the sieve up and let it hang over a bowl
> so that it drips the liquid into a bowl.
Once it has dripped the majority of the liquid, you may squeeze
> in order to place the rest of the liquid within the bowl.
You will not get copious amounts, but it is not needed.
You will then take the liquid in the bowl,
> mix it with one quarter of a cup of olive oil,
> add one drop rosemary oil,
> and place lightly upon the skin that has been affected.
You do not need great amounts.
Lightly in a circular motion, gently rub until it has penetrated the skin.
Allow at least twenty four hours
> before washing it off of the affected area.
This is to be done daily until the affectation has healed,
> has cleared away from the skin.
You will also during this process ensure that you eat daily,
> one half cup of sweet potato so that there is a twofold effort
> to assist in the healing.
And you will place upon this half cup, before you ingest,
> one quarter teaspoon ground rosemary, not cooked.
It is important that it is combined with the sweet potato,
> not placed on other food for this particular process.

250   The frangipani flower is most efficacious when dried,
> for in drying it becomes concentrated.

---

26   This does not include yams. There is difference in composition.

The fresh does not have as much efficacy,
> in this particular case, as the dried.

Once it is dried, grind it into a fine powder.
Use the dried powder as a balm
> for the eruption of herpes like sores anywhere upon the body.

In this case do not mix with water, only with olive oil.
It does not require copious amounts.
A thin layer will soothe the burning, the soreness.

251 Salal may also be used as an astringent for a wound.
You will take the leaves and cleanse the wound.
It is most efficacious along with the water.
The properties within the salal neutralize the bacteria.

252 The juice of the goji berry may be used as an antiseptic rinse
> in cases when there is none other available.

Rinse the hands before dealing with a patient with an open wound
> or open sores of any kind.

Placing the juice upon an open wound will not assist.
It may, indeed, in many cases, complicate,
> for it will attack bacteria of all sorts, including helpful bacteria.

So that is why it may be used to sterilize the hands,
> but not to be used directly in the wound.

It should not be warmed before using it
> as an antiseptic upon the hands.

You may also sterilize in cases where no other sterilization is available,
> instruments that will be used upon the being.

It may be swabbed, Soul, only within the gum area of the mouth,
> for severe infections that may be attacking,
> or in danger of attacking the brain.

In this case, it is to be the very lightest of coatings,
> placed upon the upper gum, only on the outside,
> and then rinsed quickly
> to assist in calming an infection of this matter.

253 The roots of the periwinkle may be taken up, cleansed.
> and air dried.

When all moisture has receded from the roots
> grind it into a fine powder.

This powder is most efficacious for wounds that have started to suppurate,
>   to drain and where the flesh is closing too fast.
The application of the powder will assist in removing,
>   drawing forth the poisons within the wound
>   so that it is cleansed and able to heal in an efficacious manner.
The periwinkle in its dried state may be kept as a powder,
>   in a glass jar in a dark cool place for up to eight months.
The covering on the jar is to be either a cotton or muslin
>   so that the air may circulate but the insect may not feast.
You may also, if glass is not available,
>   place within a paper, an envelope of some sort
>   or within the cloth of cotton or muslin.
In either case a cool dark area is required.

254 We would have you understand that when you take a flower
>   of the fuchsia and place it in the palm of your hand
>   and rub it with the fingertips of your other hand
>   in a clockwise motion until it becomes a glutinous mass,
>   it releases a powerful chemical.
It is most efficacious for deep infections.
Pack the gelatinous mass right in the infection.
Leave the infection open to the air.
And allow it to sit within the wound
>   for a period of at least six hours.
And then, it may be taken out and replaced with another gelatinous mass.
This is to be done every six hours for those deep severe wounds,
>   until you begin to see the wound becoming pink and healthy,
>   and the greenish cast has left.

255 The juice from garlic is most efficacious for fungus infection
>   on any part of the body.
You will take one teaspoon of garlic oil, mix with one tablespoon olive oil
>   and proceed to lightly douse the area of fungal infection with
>   this concoction.
It is to be done twice daily.

256 Soul, for a warm poultice,
>   gently heat the water to just above room temperature.
Place within the cloth a thin film of oatmeal porridge
>   made only with water.

And then, fold the cloth over and hold until the cloth cools.
Repeat three times, thrice daily.
As the wound closes,
    we would ask that the porridge is placed directly upon the flesh.
And then, the warm cloth over and held in place until the cloth cools.
Again, three times daily.

257   We would tell you of the benefits, the efficacity, of rye grass.
Indeed, Soul, for the usage that we will expound upon,
    we would have you grow it within the home.
When the stalk reaches a height of four inches, it is ready to be used.
We would suggest that you clip four leaves of grass
    and twine them together.
They are to be placed then directly within an open wound.
This will help coagulate the blood.
For extensive wounds you will place the four every four inches.
The wound will then be closed.

258   The vanilla bean, in its pure state,
    has a variety of efficacious remedies.
It is important to remove the outer shell
    and use only the internal material.
We do not recommend the outer covering in any remedy.
The vanilla bean itself, crushed[27] into a fine powder,
    is useful in the application as a talc powder,
        finely ground, placed upon the weeping sore.
The sore is not to be bandaged, covered, it is to be left open.
The powder within the vanilla bean will mix chemically
    with the weeping moisture and provide a balm to the sores.

259   The liptodorius[28] is a small yellow flower resembling the dandelion.
It is found near swamps.
It is odiferous.
It is unmistakable in its odor and that was deliberate
    so that it would be easily found and recognizable.
The leaves of this plant are the most efficacious
    in application for any sores of any type that fester.

---

27   crushed - do not crush in aluminum or with aluminum.

28   liptodorius - false dandelion

The leaves are to be chewed to a pulpy mass
    and placed upon the festering sore.
We specifically use the word, chewed,
    for it is in combination with the enzymes of the mouth
    that the efficacious properties are released.
A small ball, gummy, is all that is necessary for even a large wound.
The ball, the mass, need be no more
    than two centimeters by two centimeters.
It will be spreadable.

260   We will speak on the bright yellow marigold.
Once you have discerned the bright yellow, you will then take the petals,
    only the petals, and carefully dry them.
You will then prepare with your mortar and pestle a powder.
This powder kept within a glass container and kept dark,
    the powder will have a number of uses, depending on the dosage.
A pinch of the powder may be placed upon a wound,
    a minor scrape, to prevent infection.
It is especially beneficial for children who often scrape themselves.
The powder will neutralize the bacterium
    that would otherwise tend to reproduce themselves
    within the wound.

261   We would have you understand
    that a clove of garlic, sliced open and rubbed upon a sore
    that refuses to heal, will stimulate the healing.
This is not to be used on a sore that is oozing with infection.
This is for scar tissue in much the same way
    that your earth tells you to use vitamin E.
In many parts of the earth vitamin E is not readily available
    but garlic is and it will have the same effect.

262   A quarter cup of juniper leaves to three cups of water,
    place in boiling water, stir for one minute
    and then let sit for three minutes,
    strain and you will have a tea.
The juniper leaves that were in the boiling water
    and that you have strained out
    may be retained for a poultice,
    placed within muslin or a cheesecloth, a porous cloth.

This poultice is helpful
> where there are boils that need to be brought to a head.

In this case place the poultice after it has been heated
> upon the injury, the boil, and then allow to sit until it cools.

When it cools remove it and heat once more.
These leaves may be used up to three times for each poultice.
And thereafter, you may require fresh ones
> to be placed in the boiling water.

263 The petals of the iris may
> be used as an emollient for first degree burns.

They will have little to no effect on deeper burns,
> for they only penetrate the initial layer of the skin.

Smooth the petals of the iris until they become mushy
> and then place upon the spot that is burnt.

Allow it to sit, Soul, as you apply light pressure
> for a minimum of fifteen seconds.

Then allow it to do its work for a half an hour before you wash.

264 The properties of the cabbage family,
> specifically the red cabbage and the cauliflower,
> both have interchangeable qualities
> and so whatever is to hand will be sufficient.

The outer leaves crushed so that there is some liquid that arises;
> this liquid, Souls of earth, this moisture
> > when mixed with a teaspoon of olive oil and placed upon burns
> > will assist in the healing of burns upon the skin.

These would be first and second degree burns.
It is not efficacious for the third degree burns.
It is, Souls of earth, soothing for the sunburn,
> for in the future, Souls of earth,
> > many more will be subject to sunburn
> > as the layers, protection upon the earth fade.

265 We will speak on the bright yellow marigold.
Once you have discerned the bright yellow, you will then take the petals,
> only the petals, and carefully dry them.

You will then prepare, with your mortar and pestle, a powder.
For burns, a paste may be made of the powder,
> with olive oil as the moisture content.

The paste should be thick and placed upon the burn
>and left for a period of thirty minutes.
It may be used upon a surface burn, a second or third degree burn, also.
The olive oil should be mixed with the powder
>only to provide a paste consistency.
We would not advise making large quantities of such,
>rather we would advise that each time a new application is prepared.
This will reduce any chance of infection within the burn area.

266 For those who have access to the kelp beds,
>especially that dark, dark green,
>a handful fresh from the ocean water without being rinsed,
>placed upon the face, will heal the burns from the pollution.

Those who have skin eruptions, wherever the burns are upon the body,
>who have been burnt by the sun,
>rubbing gently of the kelp will cleanse and heal.

Soul, do not rinse first, for it is the combination of the sea salt
>and the kelp that interact with the skin and instill the healing.

267 Green tea is efficacious when cooled and applied to burns.
In the making of the tea, Souls of earth,
>use two tablespoons to one cup of water.
The tea is not to be boiled.
It is to be set within hot almost boiling water
>and allowed to sit for ten minutes.
At the end of the ten minutes, strain the water
>and place the leaves upon the burn and allow to sit
>upon the burn for five minutes for first degree burns.
For second degree burns increase the time to ten minutes.
And for third degree burns, Souls of earth, you will place the leaves
>within a natural light material before you place it upon the burn
>and allow it to seep into the burn.
In the cases of third degree burns it may sit for at least twelve minutes
>before gently removing.

268 The stems of the fireweed may be torn apart
>when the flowers no longer bloom and the inner part removed.
Dry in the sun and then grind into powder.
This powder, when mixed with olive oil, is most efficacious
>for wounds of the skin: abrasions of the skin, scrapes,
>light first degree burns, eczema, acne.

The ratio is one half teaspoon of powder to two tablespoons olive oil.
And then lightly placed on the wound, or the scrape, or the acne.

269 The roots of the fireweed is to be dried,
>then ground into a powder.

And this powder is most efficacious when placed upon
>the more severe burns, especially those burns caused by the sun,
>by high intensity of any type.

Electrical burns will respond to this.
The ground powder is to be mixed with the olive oil.
One quarter teaspoon of the powder to three tablespoons of olive oil.

270 We bring unto you, the use of macadamia nuts[29].
Particularly the oil.
Although you may grind the nut into almost a powder,
>it is the oil we are particularly interested in,
>for a one quarter teaspoon of macadamia nut oil
>with one drop rosemary applied to acne
>is very efficacious for controlling the virus break out.

Whether it be on the face or anywhere on the body,
>we would ask that you apply in a circular motion very gently.

And we ask that you rub with the two middle fingers clockwise,
>wherever upon the body.

This treatment may be repeated often during the day
>until you see improvement and then as a maintenance
>until it is gone, thrice daily.

If you use the powdered form of the nut,
>do not include that in the measurement of the one quarter teaspoon.

It must be measured oil without the powder.
We have no objection to adding some of the nut powder
>for it will relieve any itching, but we ask that if you do this,
>it is done after the initial measurement
>and it is no more than one sixteenth of the teaspoon.

271 We have for you a use for the geranium.
Only the petals, not the leaves or the stem.
The deeper the color the more efficacious.
It is, Soul, for those beings who have the acne.
You will take the petals until one half cup.

---

29 Caution: use only oil from Macadamia integrifolia and Macadamia tetraphylla.

Rinse each one so that there is no dirt.
It is necessary that they be clean of dirt.
Once you have cleansed the petals immerse them in water.
The water is to cover the petals.
And place this in the sun with a cloth over the top
> so that no dirt will enter,
>> but the warmth of the sun will heat and stimulate the petals.

Leave it out in the sun for two hours.
At the end of the two hours, strain the water and place it aside.
Take the petals and grind them until they become pasty like.
And then take the water you put aside and stir in the petals.
Blend, stirring heartily, and as soon as you stop the stirring,
> take the top layer and place it upon the acne.

Stir again, take the top layer and place it upon the acne.
You do not need a lot, but you do need to do it
> only after you have stirred, and the top layer.

Wherever the acne is upon the body
> place and leave on for fifteen minutes.

This may be done three times daily.
Once the acne has begun to leave it will only be necessary to do this
> every other day until the acne is totally gone.

272 For the acne, smooth the petals of the iris between the fingers
> until they become mushy and then place upon the acne spot.

Push lightly in so that the moisture penetrates the skin,
> and hold it there for a minimum of twelve seconds.

Try not to wash the area for a period of twenty five minutes
> to allow it to continue penetration.

In cases where there are large areas, place enough petals
> that you may fill your hand and then hold your hand
> against the flesh that is afflicted with the acne
> for the same amount of time.

And again, try not to wash the area for a period of twenty five minutes
> to allow it to continue penetration.

273 We would speak on the properties of the cabbage family,
> specifically the red cabbage and the cauliflower.

Both have interchangeable qualities
> and so whatever is to hand will be sufficient.

The flower is of use in powdered form.

Remove all moisture and then air dry it until it becomes crumbly
>   and then grind that into a fine powder.

It is useful for the acne anywhere upon the body as a wash,
>   one teaspoon to one quart of water.

In the cases of the acne, allow it to dry
>   and leave it upon the skin until your next wash.

274 The leaves of the daisy at full bloom,
>   for the leaves are also affected by the condition of the flower,
>   may be efficacious in the treatment of acne.

You may take the leaves, curl them up, roll them up into a small ball;
>   three leaves will suffice for a full acne problem of the face.

For the torso, another three.

For the bottom, another three.

These are to be squished and then rubbed into the flesh clockwise,
>   wherever the acne appears.

There will be minute, almost unrecognizable moisture felt by the skin
>   but it is enough to relieve and to cure the acne.

You may place the leaves in an airtight container for future use.

They keep very well in a dark place, away from direct sunlight.

275 We would have you understand the inner peel of a banana
>   may be efficacious in cases where the facial, and we stress facial,
>   eruptions can not be controlled.

Where the acne, pimple, have not responded.

We would ask that you take the inner portion
>   and rub it gently upon the affected areas of the face[30].

It is most efficacious.

For those whose acne is filtered throughout their body in various places,
>   we would ask that you place upon the inner peel of the banana
>   one drop of olive oil, one drop of geranium oil,
>   and then rub gently upon those other areas of the body
>   that have the acne, or any derivative related to the acne.

If the oil of geranium is not available you may use crushed petals
>   of the geranium, six in number, along with the olive oil.

276 We would speak of the deep purple clematis for roseola.

Three petals rubbed together so that they stick together

---

30   of the face - it is to be left on to dry, before rinsing with clear water, not soap. Or you may rinse it with olive oil.

and then placed upon wherever the roseola is, rubbed gently in,
allowed to stay for fifteen minutes before wiping away.
Three treatments will relieve the roseola.
The treatments are to be done thrice daily
for three days, one after the other.
Day one, day two, day three.
No separation of days, for if you separate the days you must begin again.
The petals may be dried.
After they are dried, grind them up to form the powder.
To use as powder for roseola,
one quarter teaspoon mixed with a drop or two of olive oil,
and applied gently to the roseola area and
allowed to stay for fifteen minutes before wiping away.

277 A help with rashes.
Cease, stop using soap for wash.
Bathe the feet, the soles, the toes, the heel in chamomile tea.
Allow the tea to steep for a minimum of six minutes.
Allow the tea to cool to room temperature
and bathe the feet for ten minutes.
The placing of vitamin E oil, which may be taken from capsule,
upon the flushing of the body will help alleviate the symptoms.

278 We would discuss the properties of strawberry leaves:
ten leaves of the strawberry placed within a half cup of water,
allowed to sit in the sun for a period of three days,
and then you may strain the leaves out of the water
and use the water for all manner of eczema upon the body.
And you may ingest the water three times daily, especially in cases
where the eczema covers more than one tenth of the body mass.

279 The bud of the strawberry before it ripens is also useful
but in a different capacity.
This small berry bud, picked before it begins to turn color
may be used as a tea for the body.
It is not the ripe strawberries we speak of, it is the green.
That is where the properties are most efficacious for application to the body.
For one cup of tea take six of the green buds, steep in hot water
five minutes.
It does not have to be boiling.
Strain the buds, cool the liquid and then apply the tea.

The resulting liquid is to be used
> for those severe cases of eczema and psoriasis.

For it will not burn the open sores but will help to soothe the open sores.
You may pour the liquid directly upon the affected area
> and know it will be soothing.

Do not wash.
Allow it to air dry and it may be used upon any part of the body afflicted.

280   For the being who has skin cracked and broken from the eczema
> you may place upon the cracks the water from the infusion
> and rub it into the cracks, and it will soothe.

The infusion comprised of three parts water to one part pure spearmint
> so that, Soul, if you have three tablespoons of water
> you will have one tablespoon pure spearmint leaves.

If it is dry pure spearmint, you will make it one and a half tablespoons.
Place within the water and let sit for a period of no more than six hours.
This infusion may be stored within a cool area of darkness
> for no more than thirty days.

281   A thin slice of the bark of the juniper is to be dried
> and then ground into a fine powder.

This powder when mixed with the olive oil is efficacious for eczema
> that will respond to no other treatment.

It is to be laved upon the afflicted area and allowed to dry
> and only when completely dry may the powder be brushed off

282   For those who have access to the kelp beds,
> especially that dark, dark green
> we draw your attention to the bulb.

Indeed, for within the bulb are healing properties as a lotion
> that may be smoothed upon the skin
> for the days when the sun is intense
> and there is little shade or covering.

The babe will benefit greatly from smoothing it
> upon the exposed skin especially,
> when there is a burning sun
> because of the environmental damage to the earth.

283   We would speak of the lily, the deep orange, the golden orange,
> or the white ones.

The leaves of the lily are of great value when crushed within the hands
    and kneaded with the fingers until they become pulpy.
You may then place it upon any incidence of poison ivy,
    or any like nettle rash.
It will immediately soothe the burning and the itching,
    and prevent the eruption of the blisters in the case of the nettle,
    and prevent the rash of the poison ivy or the poison sumac,
    or any poisonous leaf from extending its effect upon the body.
You will leave, Soul, the moisture from the pulpiness to dry.
It is not to be washed off if at all possible for the length of three hours.
Then it may be washed away and you may apply a new leaf if necessary.

284 We would speak on the properties of the cabbage family,
    specifically the red cabbage and the cauliflower.
Both have interchangeable qualities
    and so whatever is to hand will be sufficient.
The flower is of use in powdered form.
Remove all moisture and then air dry it until it becomes crumbly
    and then grind that into a fine powder.
Mix one teaspoon to one quart of water.
For those who suffer from the itching of the scabies or like bacterial insects,
    an application of this mixture once every three hours
    will alleviate the itching.

285 We would give forth a remedy for itching, for eruptions.
We would have you understand that the beeswax
    is especially efficacious.
When added to this remedy, the wax will assist
    in holding onto the skin the remedy.
And so within one quarter cup of olive oil, place one drop peppermint,
    one teaspoon melted beeswax, one drop of bergamot,
    one drop jasmine.
It is to be warmed so that the wax is melted,
    not boiling, Soul,
    and then allowed to cool to skin temperature
    before placing upon the being.
You will, Souls of earth, in this particular remedy
    mix vigorously to a cream.

286 The petals of the deep purple clematis may be dried.
Grind them up to form the powder.
Two teaspoons of the powder mixed in
  with one quarter teaspoon to one quarter cup of cold cream,
  or you may use olive oil.
This concoction is most efficacious for an itchy rash.
This is not to be used with a rash
  that is cracked open or has a leaking sore.
Rub it on the rash and it will relieve.
The itchiness will respond to the gentle rubbing and you will, Soul,
  reapply whenever necessary until the rash has receded
  and the itch has left.
You may continue to apply even after the itch has ceased,
  until the rash itself is gone.

287 It is most helpful for the little babe who has the diaper rash.
Ten leaves of the strawberry placed within a half cup of water,
  allowed to sit in the sun for a period of three days,
  and then you may strain the leaves out of the water.
The placing of this water upon their being is most efficacious.
Allow the water to gently pour over the affected area.
Do not wipe it away.
Merely let it be.

288 We would give forth a remedy for skin eruptions that have
  as symptoms burning, also symptoms of weeping;
    the sore will weep.
We would suggest that the remedy be used sparingly.
It is not necessary to place copious amounts.
The remedy will consist of one fourth cup olive oil
  mixed within one drop of lavender,
    one drop barberry juice, one drop of bergamot.
This is to set in a dark spot for one hour before placing upon the skin.
It may be placed upon the skin three times per day.
This will alleviate the burning and assist the skin to heal.
It may be placed anywhere upon the body that has an eruption,
  any that has burning attached.
That is the key, for it is meant to soothe the burning
  and allow stimulus of healing to take place.
If it burns, Soul, that is the key.

289 The fruit of the plantain, ground unto the point of liquidity,
    is also efficacious for the dry skin,
        especially skin that is cracking from dryness,
        from the effect of disease.
Mix one teaspoon of the liquid to one teaspoon of the olive oil
    and then place upon the painful skin that has cracked.
Oft times, throughout each day place wherever the skin has cracked.
This will assist the skin to heal itself and cease to be painful.
And this is the case for the child and the adult.

290 We would speak today on the properties of sedge.
Much sedge is found in places of moisture.
Clippings from the sedge may be used as a balm,
    for those beings who have had to enter out into the sunshine
    and their skin has erupted from contact,
        lengthy contact with the sun.
To place clippings and the mud within which it grows upon the soreness
    is efficacious for this type of sunburn.
Placed upon the skin burnt by the rays
    for a total of twelve earth minutes until it begins to cake and dry
    and then you may rinse off.
If the sores are not opened and weeping, you may use again but not
    if the sores are open.
Then it must be discarded and new used the next time.

291 We would have you understand the leaves of the peony
    make a most excellent emollient for the skin.
Take a minimum of seven petals from the flower
    and two leaves while they are moist.
Do not, Soul, do this with dried,
    for it will chafe your hands, not help them.
Then rub between your hands the petals and the two leaves.
And gently keep rubbing until you have the moistness from the plant
    transferred to the palms of your hand.
And then, you may rub the backs of your hands and move the petals
    up and down your arms, even unto your cheeks.
And you will find them soothed.
The chemical from the leaves and the petals of the peony
    will enter in to your skin and provide relieve from dryness.

They will also, Soul, in a larger amount,
> rubbed upon the face, protect against the rays of the sun.

You will understand the peonies are only to be used
> during the growth season.

Drying them out removes the benefit.

292   The primrose has many uses.
The primrose is most efficacious for the young skin,
> as a protective barrier for sun and wind.

Take the petals and place them in a container.
As you are placing the petals within, rub them
> and drop them from a height above,
>> for this stimulates the natural oils, the natural aromatics
> and the natural healing from the primrose.

Fill the container to at least two and a half inches,
> and then let sit for twenty four hours;
>> at least three of those hours in sunshine.

It must, Soul, have direct sunshine for that period.
The following day you will crunch the petals
> until they have become a mass.

There will be some moisture left,
> not much but enough that they will hold together.

Crunching them in an up and down movement
> will not bring forward the full vibration.

It has to be in a clockwise circle that you do this.
Once you have this mass, add one teaspoon of water,
> and then proceed to mix until you have blended
> what is left of the petals and the water.

This concoction may then be rubbed upon the exposed skin of a child,
> and it will give them protection
> for as long as they do not wash it off.

You will not be required to rub hard,
> it is enough to gently place upon the body.

293   The wallflower is most efficacious when the leaves,
> four at a time are taken
> and placed in no more than two tablespoons of water,
> that is slightly warmed by the sun.

This will sit for a period of twelve minutes.
The water from the leaves is placed upon sores that have blistered,
> then the leaves placed over the water.

The leaves are left for a period of three minutes,
  allowing it to soak into the skin.
This may be repeated three times daily.

294 The cayenne pepper is efficacious
  in the treatment of poison ivy before the sores have opened.
Once the sores have opened, this is not efficacious.
In the initial state of the poison ivy, or indeed the poison oak,
  it will prevent the opening up of the skin.
Soothing over the affected area and then washing off is all that is required.

295 One teaspoon of macadamia nut oil[31] with one drop lavender oil,
  is efficacious for the lactating mother to soothe the breasts.

296 This mixture may be used for those
  who have difficulty healing chapped skin:
one teaspoon macadamia nut oil with one drop lavender oil.

297 We would speak on warts.
In order to rid the being of warts,
  we would have you understand both a topical application
  and an ingestion, simultaneously.
You will mix for the topical application,
  one half teaspoon baking soda, one quarter teaspoon olive oil
  with one drop rosemary.
This is to be placed upon each wart and held for at least
  eight seconds and no more than twelve before it is removed.
As an adjunct to ridding the body of this virus,
  ingest daily one half teaspoon ground rosemary.
This may be placed upon food.

298 We would speak on the properties of the lily, not all lilies,
  only the ones who have the deep orange, the golden orange,
  or the white ones.
The petals are most efficacious in healing warts,
  whether they be on the soles of the feet, or on the body parts.
In those cases where those petals are to be used
  you will leave them in place upon the wart for a period of one hour.

---

31 Caution: use only oil from Macadamia integrifolia and Macadamia tetraphylla.

Take the petal,
> knead it with your fingers in the palm of your hand,
> until moisture begins to appear, until you feel a bit of moisture.

At that point its properties are being released
> and it may be placed upon the wart and held in place.

This is to be done twice daily until the wart has left.
It has, Soul, properties to draw out.

299 The petals of the flower liptodorius[32] have a very different efficacy
> and are used for wart removal.

They will draw out the virus and deflate and inhibit the growth of a wart.
The petals are to be dried, ground, mixed with a minute amount
> of olive oil to give it consistency and then placed upon the wart.

A bandage will be placed over for a period of three to ten days.
The length of time will vary
> according to the health of the individual and to the size of the wart.

Each day a clean bandage and petals
> should be reapplied for optimum efficacy.

300 We would speak of the properties of the daffodil.
The stem of the daffodil is efficacious as a lotion for dryness.
The mere rubbing together of a portion of the stem,
> releases properties into the skin which assist in emolliating dryness.

It may be used upon any portion of the body but is recommended
> and efficacious for the hands and the feet.

It is helpful in removing the rough callous for those who would do so.
The stem is to be used as is.

301 For those who have access to the kelp beds,
> especially that dark, dark green,
> we draw your attention to the bulb
> for those who have leprosy like symptoms within the body.

Within the bulb, you will take a dab and place on the tongue,
> not under the tongue, on the tongue.

This is to be done over a three day period once every hour,
> and it will stimulate the immune system to fight off the dregs
> of leprosy like disease.

Most efficacious, the strongest, are the bulbs of the dark, dark green.

---

32 liptodorius - false dandelion

The others, Soul, in varying colors are also efficacious,
>but not as strong and they would take more time to assist the body.

Systemic
302 We speak on the properties of the heliotrope.
It is of great assistance to those beings
>in the throes of withdrawal, especially withdrawal
>of your cannabis, of your mescal, of your heroin.
It is the petals that will give you the most efficacity.
You will pick them first thing in the morning.
Five petals is all that is required three times a day.
You will take the five petals in the morning right after being picked
>and you will mush them between your fingers and
>place them on the tongue and allow it to sit on the tongue
>as you deep breathe in and out five times, slowly.
Breath in.
Hold for the count of three.
Breathe out for the count of four.
And then remove the petals and put them aside.
Within five hours to six hours you will again take five petals
>and repeat the process, mushing them, placing on the tongue
>and then breathing and taking them out
>and putting them aside with the first five petals.
And then within three hours you will take another five petals.
The same procedure, the mush, placing on the tongue, the breathing.
And then you will take them out
>and put them together with the first ten petals.
You will now have a gob
>and within one hour you will take and place that gob within
>and you will chew it.
You will not swallow it, Soul.
You will chew it to get the healing
>that will enter in and assist you in the withdrawal.
Once you have chewed no more than fifteen times,
>you will remove that and you have finished for that day.
This is not to be done on a daily basis.
During the withdrawal process it is enough to do it thrice weekly,
>but it will be of great efficacity for your being.

303 We will speak on the properties of steam
    and its effect upon the human body.
In a quart of boiling water placing two drops anise
    is most efficacious for those beings who are in,
    entering in to withdrawal from drug of any kind[33].
    except for the heroin.
Allow, Soul, the room to be a small one
    wherein the steam may escape near the patient
    and waft the odor unto the being's consciousness.

304 We bring unto you an exercise
    to increase the speed of releasing toxins from your body.
This is applicable to those who are coming off drugs,
    those who have stopped smoking,
    those who have ingested accidentally a poison,
    those beings who eat flesh with pesticides.
This exercise, to be efficacious, to increase the speed of releasing the toxins,
    to increase the speed at which you heal, must be done three times daily.
Each time facing east.

Step 1
At the level of the heart place together your palms,
    fingers touching fingers, thumbs touching thumbs,
    the thumbs held in an upright position.

Step 2
Breathe deeply in through the nostrils.
Hold for the count of three and release slowly for the count of three.

Step 3
Breathe deeply in through the nostrils.
Hold for the count of three and release slowly for the count of four.
Step 4
Once again breathe deeply in through the nostrils.
Hold for the count of three and release slowly for the count of six.

Step 5
Maintaining the position of the hands and the fingers,

---

33 withdrawal from drug of any kind - referring to prescribed drugs.

you will turn your thumbs toward your body
and bring the hands up unto the throat chakra area.
And you will hold that position for the count of five,
breathing slowly and regularly.

Step 6
Move your hands upward,
maintaining the position of the thumb towards the body
until you have reached the position of the third eye.
The thumbs will be directly in front of the third eye,
bring them forward so that they touch the third eye.
and hold that position for the count of five.

Step 7
Breath in deeply through the nostrils,
hold and at the end of the count of five,
forcefully exhale in one breath, whiiiish,
making the sound of the word, wish.

Step 8
Move your thumbs away from the third eye,
slowly bringing your hands downward back to the position
in front of the heart with the thumbs upright
and the fingers in front of the flesh.

Step 9
Bring your hands downward and slowly
move your fingers and thumbs away from each other.
Place your hands palm up and you have finished.

305 We would speak now on the properties
of the internal of the daffodil flower.
This powdery substance when touched,
may be placed directly upon the tongue.
Merely a dab and this will assist in any ailment
caused by restriction of the vein or artery.
Therefore it may be efficacious in the treatment of the headache,
of the stroke, of those who have the difficulty of the dystrophy
and the sclerosis and the ALS.

306 The leaves of the holly tree are especially efficacious
  but only the center part of the leaves
  and only those leaves that have reached two years or more of growth.
Before two years of growth have occurred,
  there will be little sap that will enter in to the leaves.
Take the center part of the leaf
  to no more than one centimeter from the edge,
  grind the leaf unto its smallest portion that you can,
  and then leave it to dry.
When it is dried, once again grind it until it becomes a powdery substance.
This powdery substance may then be placed within a liquid.
The liquid will only be used to assist the ingestion of the powder.
It may also be mixed with the honey in order for the ingestion to be easy.
For those who have Aids it would also be efficacious
  to imbibe some of the ground leaf,
  one eighth teaspoon three times daily for a period of three days.
That is the extent to which the ingestion should take place.

307 The holly tree has within it the properties to help
  in the eruption of sores caused by any immune deficiency;
  the outer bark of the holly tree, a small one by one inch square
  placed within one fourth cup water and allowed to sit for three days.
So those who have Aids, for example,
  will be helped by this water placed upon eruptions.
Those who have herpes may also use the water to bathe the afflicted areas,
  this will soothe the burning and the pain,
  and stimulate the body to heal.

308 Indeed, plants assist in wellness, in cleansing the air.
But, Soul, there is no place left of pure air.
We recommend where possible, the plant you call spider plant.
For it is a workhorse of cleansing, of helping to clear the air of toxins.
We would also recommend where possible the palm tree, indoors,
  for an immediate benefit.
In the areas of coldness, the maple is of great efficacity
  in its filtering ability.
There is another plant that we would recommend for the indoors
  to assist the spider plant and that is a philodendron.
The philodendron must be placed high.
It is not a plant that works best on a short table.

The leaves may be trained to circle the room
    and cleanse the air in the upper sections.
This would also be good in the room where sleep takes place.

309 We would suggest, Souls of earth, that when you have an allergy
    do not fully cover your floors with your carpet.
Small carpets cleaned often are acceptable.
We would have you understand your carpets are harbingers, are carriers,
    are holders of many of your ailments
    related to allergies, to flu, to colds.
They are magnets for microbes that might be harmful.

310 We will speak on allergies.
It is to bring to the attention of humanity the effect of the toxins
    upon the land, upon the air and within the body.
Allergies in themselves do not cause illness.
They are the effect of illness, of the illness of the planet,
    of the illness of the parent that carries the child.
Allergies developed later on in life are a result of toxic invasion
    that has built to the point where the physical being
    must either release it or develop cancerous tumour growth.
That treatment for allergy, when due to bacteria, will have no effect.
When the treatment is given for the bacteria, then it will be efficacious
    but when it is treated as an allergy, it is not efficacious.
One quarter teaspoon ground seaweed in algae form
    will be beneficial to the control of excess bacteria within the system.
We would caution only green algae.
For those who have already an excess of bacterium within the being,
    one teaspoon three times daily for a period of seven days
    will bring the system back into its balance
    and thereafter, the ingestion daily of half a teaspoon will be sufficient.

311 We would have you understand the uses are many and varied
    of the plant called tansy.
But always within the constraints given,
    for tansy has an opportunity to become toxic when overused.
And therefore, we caution that you follow exactly the parameters given.
The tansy tea may be efficacious
    as an anti inflammatory and anti phlegm concoction.
In this case, Soul, we would ask that the flower not be used.

That one leaf, at least two and a half inches from point
> to the end of the leaf, be placed in two cups boiling water.

The leaf then to be removed after five minutes
> and the water may be sipped slowly throughout the day.

No more than one quarter cup will be necessary per day.

312   We would speak on the properties of the pansy.
We would have you understand the leaves of this plant are efficacious
> for those who have the rheumatoid arthritis.

In its beginning stages of the disease, the ingestion of three leaves,
> thrice daily, will assist in ridding the toxins
> of this disease from the body.

The leaves, to be most efficacious, must be fresh.
In a dried form you will use three times the amount,
> ingest, dried, nine leaves three times daily.

The dried concoction may be mixed in purified water, warm, not boiling.
It is not for a tea.
It is only placed in water to enable the being to drink it.

313   The odor of pine is most efficacious for those beings
> who find themselves prone to arthritic and rheumatoid arthritis.

It is to be three drops oil of pine to one quart boiling water,
> and allow the aroma to waft over the being
> and it will soothe the pain as the moisture enters in
> and is absorbed by the skin.

It will not cease the pain, Souls, but it will ameliorate.

314   We would speak on the rheumatoid arthritic,
> those whose joints have become gnarled and distorted.

This is for the later stages for relief.
We would have you, Soul, make a compound beginning with
> one half teaspoon baking soda,
> add to it one quarter teaspoon cream of tartar,
>> mix in one quarter teaspoon olive oil, one quarter teaspoon honey
>> and two drops rosemary, one drop lavender.

Gently lave onto the gnarled members the compound.
Allow it to set at least fifteen seconds
> before removal for the first application.

Within one hour, you will do the second application.
Leave it on for twelve minutes before removal.

And then, Souls of earth, within one hour repeat the first application.
This is to be done daily until you notice a reduction in pain
      and in many cases a beginning straightening of the member.
Once that occurs you will need to apply only once daily,
      for the twelve minutes.
And you may, Souls of earth, continue with the once daily
      to hold at bay the pain, and the stiffness, and the distortion.

315   Souls who are attempting to overcome, who are fighting a flu
      and related viruses and bacteria, will benefit
      from the application of the olive oil massage to the feet;
      one tablespoon olive oil with the addition of one drop of lavender.
And correspondingly the same is also applied across the upper chest.
Again, Souls, a minute amount.
This will bring relief and enhance the immune system to combat.

316   Soul, daily application of olive oil, lightly,
      to the palms of your hands and to the palms of your feet,
      this is preventative and helps in the balancing of your being.
Indeed it is a balm to the spirit and to the flesh.

317   We would speak on the properties of the rose.
We would caution that all information is to be utilized
      from the flower, from the plant that is without taint
      of pesticide, herbicide, or growth hormones.
All of those chemicals will prevent the efficacy of the remedy.
We would approach, first, the root of the rose bush.
We would suggest the snipping of one quarter inch
      near the base of the stem.
Not within the root ball,
      but within three inches near the base of the stem.
The piece you have snipped will be cleansed in cold water.
Hot water will dilute the effects of the remedy.
Air dry the piece and then grind into a fine powder.
It is not to be refrigerated or placed in a heating mechanism.
The resultant ground powder may then be used,
      to stop bleeding as in your styptic pencil.
It is to be used for small wounds.
It may be used upon the human or upon the animal,
      it is efficacious to all.

It will cease the bleeding and perform the activities of an antibiotic.
It is especially useful for scrapes of childhood.
It will promote the healing of skin over the small wound.

318 We will speak on the properties of the leaves of the rose bush.
These are to be allowed to drop to such a state
    where they may be crumbled easily by touch.
They are not to be refrigerated in a cold place.
They require tepid air to dry and not affect the potency.
The crumbled leaves may be mixed with honey as a paste
    and applied to boils and carbuncles.
This remedy will withdraw the infection, the pus from the flesh.
The placement of the paste is to be changed frequently
    and cleansed before the placement of further paste.
We suggest the placement is done every hour
    until the infection has ceased to inflame the flesh.
It is, Soul, a topical antibiotic with properties that enter the flesh
    for the antiseptic cleansing of the area infected.

319 The frangipani flower is most efficacious for the young babe
    who is subject to eruptions of boils and or sores like boils.
The frangipani flower is most efficacious when dried,
    for in drying it becomes concentrated.
The fresh does not have as much efficacy,
    in this particular case, as the dried.
Once it is dried, grind it into a fine powder.
In this case you will make a poultice of the powder;
    a half teaspoon mixed with one tablespoon of olive oil,
        placed upon the eruption and then a warm cloth placed over,
    for a minimum of one half hours.
If there is no cloth able to be warmed
    then place your hand and hold it there so that the warmth
    may assist the healing properties to be released.
At the end of the half hour, you may then wipe it off.

320 The stamen of the fireweed is particularly efficacious
    when made powdery, ground with your fingers.
Those who have difficulty with burning of the limbs
    due to neuropathy or any nervous system disease,
    may benefit from a light coating of this powder
    upon the affected members.

If it is the feet then it is to be placed on the bottom of the feet.
If it is upon the hands, the arms, the upper torso,
    it is rubbed in and left to naturally dissipate.

321 For the being plagued with bursitis,
    we would have you bring together the petals of
    three dandelion flowers and crunch them within your palm
    and then place them in a bowl with five drops olive oil
    for three flowers.
Grind until it becomes a congealed mass and place it upon the area
    of the bursitis and allow it to penetrate the skin.
Hold it on, or allow it to rest
    upon the area of the bursitis for fifteen minutes.
Collect the congealed mass and then again place it in your palm,
    place your other palm over it, massage it, warm it up
    and then place it on the back of your neck and hold it there,
    whether by your hand or by a cloth for fifteen minutes
    and then remove the mass and you will know
    that you have already received much relief.

322 The leaves of the holly tree are especially efficacious
    but only the center part of the leaves
    and only those leaves that have reached
    two years or more of growth.
Before two years of growth have occurred,
    there will be little sap that will enter in to the leaves.
Taking the center part of the leaf to no more than one centimeter
    from the edge,
        you will grind the leaf unto its smallest portion that you can,
        and then leave it to dry.
When it is dried, once again grind it
    until it becomes a powdery substance.
This powdery substance may then be placed within a liquid.
The liquid will only be used to assist the ingestion of the powder.
It may also be mixed with the honey
    in order for the ingestion to be easy.
One eighth teaspoon for an adult ingested once daily
    for three days will assist
        in overcoming Candida, any yeast infection,
        anywhere upon the body.
A few grams is all that is necessary for any one under the age of ten.

Mixed with a bit of honey, the same powder may be applied
      to those areas of the body wherever the eruption shows externally.
So you have a twofold application, the ingestion
      and on the body for those eruptions of soreness due to the fungus.

323   We would have you understand your lips,
      and the sounds that utter forth with them have power
      to assist in your well being.
Flutter your lips, brrrrr, brrrrr, brrrrr three times,
      and it will recall to your mind the need to calm your being.
It is a nudge that you may give yourself.

324   We would speak of the properties of the rose.
We find most efficacious that which you call wild roses,
      those that were placed here in their original state
      and before they became hybrid.
For the wild roses contain the most Energy and are the most efficacious.
You may use the petals of the rose to assist in calming the nerves.
Hold within each palm seven petals.
Hold lightly, place the fingers over the petals and feel the calmness enter in.
And then, deep breath and relax.

325   Indeed, the Ritalin masks.
And in addition to masking, it exacerbates.
It causes a detrimental reaction within the synapses within the brain,
      which may not show any effect for many years.
It is an insidious chemical.
The effect of calming the being is not the problem,
      for the being will be calm in a calm environment.
It is the cacophony of sound that reverberates within the being
      as if you had drank too much caffeine and the nerves jangle.
And so, the being is always on edge in an environment of noise.
The being must meditate to overcome and relax the self.
Ritalin is a solution indeed, but you must consider the long term effects
      and it is not one we recommend,
      although you are free to choose for the child.
We would suggest a daily practice to eventually overcome the sensitivity.
Sit upright in a chair with arms preferably,
      in a room silent except for the very low playing of ocean waves.

Concentrate on the ocean waves, on the sound,
>   bringing them in unto the child until they become
>   part and parcel of the child, daily, fifteen minutes minimum.
And eventually the child will be able to recall the peace of the ocean waves
>   whenever the child requires it.
This will help the child to filter out.
We would also have you understand the being has been plagued
>   by what you would term as normal sound, to the child is loud,
>   what you would term as normal lighting, to the child is bright light.
The sunglasses need not be dark, dark.
They may require only the lightest of shading.
It will be enough.

326 We would address the ameliorating
>   of a cancer for those afflicted with such.
Massage four times daily with the application
>   both feet, top and bottom, including the ankles.
Mix within one quarter cup olive oil,
>   the one drop oil of geranium, one drop oil of lavender,
>   one drop oil of chamomile, and one drop rosemary oil.
This will alert the body to healing.
It is important that the inner ankles are especially massaged
>   with the remedy for a period of thirty seconds, four times daily.

327 Soul, we will speak on the properties of the daisy.
A plant that is being altered through experimental science,
>   a plant that is being genetically modified.
We speak only of the daisy that has not been altered,
>   that is of the old seed pods, wild,
>   and those that have been carefully cultivated and preserved.
The petals are to be plucked from the head of the flower
>   when it is at its peak of bloom.
If they are plucked before it is in full bloom the efficacy will be affected.
If you wait until the bloom begins to droop,
>   the efficacy will be affected also.
We would have you know that six petals,
>   squished together, dried and ground into a fine powder,
>   will be efficacious in the treatment of certain cancerous diseases.
Any cancers of the skin, especially those cancers,
>   those tumors that attack the inner webbing of the fingers,

the toes or the backs of the knees or the inner elbow,
those that affect the back of the earlobe,
these will respond to the powder being placed upon that area.
In the case of the powder of the daisy, it is twofold remedy.
There is the placement of the powder, rubbing into the flesh,
and there is the placement of two fingers,
dabbing into the powder and placing on the tongue.
This is to be done three times daily.
Should the tumors be of a size beyond five centimeters,
the dosage will be increased to a minimum of six times a day.
The petals may not be dried in the stove,
the heating element, the microwave.
They are to be air dried.
Once made into powder they may be placed in a glass container
and you will separate that which is to be used
to be rubbed into the flesh and that which is to be on the tongue.
It is only a precaution.

328 Six florets of the pink sedum ground into a fine powder
is most efficacious for the beings who are afflicted with Aids
and cancer of the blood.
The sedum is air dried and finely ground to a powder form.
Place one tablespoon to half quart of water.
Divide the half quart into threes
then finish one each day for three days.
This is to be sipped slowly every day throughout the day.
Continue this remedy for a period of ten days.
On the tenth day, Souls, should you feel the healing beginning
within your being and a strengthening of your being
and a lifting of your being, you may cease.
If not, Souls, we would suggest you continue for a full fifteen days.
Thereafter, once you know the healing process has begun and taken hold
then you will require this remedy only one third every three days.
So that a third of a quart will last nine days.
It is not necessary to refrigerate,
but we would recommend a cool dark place
for the remedy during its ingestion period.

329 We would suggest, Souls of earth, the aroma of the oil of jasmine
is most efficacious for a being undergoing chemotherapy.

> To have it nearby during the full process,
> and directly after within the half hour after it is finished.

330 Taking the juniper berries of this bush,
> six berries are placed in boiled water
> and allowed to steep for three minutes.
Take the tea made from the berries,
> mixed with two teaspoons olive oil.
This remedy is efficacious for those who suffer tendinitis,
> your carpal tunnel or any related stress,
> strain upon the muscles, the sinews of the body.
It is to be placed upon the afflicted area, massaged in, and left to dry.
During the drying period there will be no activity of the afflicted limbs
> whether it is hands or arms, or feet or legs; they are to remain still.
And then as it is dried, you may resume normal activity.

331 The feet carry the body.
They also carry a chakra.
It is important to keep the daily activity of olive oil upon the feet.
Massage gently olive oil, daily.
Especially concentrate on the center of the soles of your feet,
> applying a light pressure in a circular motion clockwise
> seven times on each foot.
This will result in a number of effects,
> one of which is increased enhancement
> of the circulation of your body,
> another of which is the awakening of that chakra to a greater extent.
Another is not just the circulation, but the connection to the heart,
> and so it will also stimulate the heart.
We would ask, Soul, that at the end of the seventh revolution
> that you also apply lightly olive oil to the ankles.

332 For those beings who have an affliction of circulation,
> we would recommend berries of the juniper bush concoction
> to be used upon the soles of the feet.
Taking six berries of the juniper bush, place in boiled water
> and allowed to steep for three minutes of your earth.
Take the tea made from the berries, mix with two teaspoons olive oil,
> and massage it into the soles of the feet,
> remembering the heels and the toes,
> and allow it to dry.

The feet are to be raised up while the concoction is drying upon the being.
For severe cases of circulation problems,
> this is to be done every three hours until sleep time.

And continued until circulation improves.
For less severe cases once every six hours
> will suffice, again until circulation improves.

333   The cold virus, when it settles into the muscles,
> affects the production of the lactic acid, increasing the disturbance
> to the muscle system causing the swelling upon the nerves.

Indeed, it is part of the process.
We would suggest that you place poultice upon the back
> and hold it there for five minutes, rest for fifteen,
> and place back on for five,
> rest for fifteen and once more for five.

And you will do this thrice daily until the stiffness is altered.
The poultice is comprised of one teaspoon
> of what you call prepared mustard.

Place within the mustard
> one drop rosemary oil, one drop lavender oil
> before you place it within a wet cloth.

You will spread this concoction thinly upon the cloth.
No more than five minutes each time.
As you become unstiff, we would suggest that you indulge
> in moderate activity to refresh the memory of the muscles.

Thrice daily, five minutes each time a continuous walk, then you may rest.
We request that you walk, even when pain is intense,
> it is imperative to walk,
> to keep all that works within the muscles, to keep the muscles elastic.

You will notice within three days an improvement.
Remember, Soul, the lanolin[34] in between each application.
The emollient of the lanolin not only soothes the skin
> but provides a road into the muscles for the mustard;
> only to be done until the easing of pain.

334   All colors of yellow have efficacious properties.
In the very palest of yellow when there is just a tinge,
> when it looks almost white;
> this is the color to use with babies for a restful sleep.

---

34 lanolin - In the lotion, add three parts lavender oil to one part jasmine oil.

It is not for colicky babies, that is another color.
It is for those babies that never seem to be fully still as they are asleep.
Bundle the child within this color, preferably in a natural material
    and place nearby ribbons of this color upon the sleeping area.
Three ribbons, six inches,
    held together by the fourth ribbon and placed nearby.
The fluttering of the ribbon by the slightest of breezes
    whether manmade or natural from the wind,
    will set off a vibration of soothing for the child.
If there is no wind, gently waft the ribbons so that they move.
The motion will be efficacious.

335 For vertigo, for all symptoms, phases of dizziness, of nausea,
    a mixture of star anise and the ginger root
    is efficacious in its application.
The seeds of anise ground into fine sand like grains,
    slivers of ginger root sliced fine, minuscule.
Mix up to one quarter teaspoon; one eighth anise, one eighth ginger.
A quarter teaspoon of the mixture ingested every half hour
    until the symptoms recede.
It may be mixed with honey,
    it may be placed in a cool liquid,
    or it may be ingested dry.
For simple cases of nausea or slight dizziness,
    two applications and no more is sufficient.
For those suffering from vertigo where the world will not cease to spin,
    it will be necessary to continue a dosage
        for a minimum of six times before the symptoms begin to recede.
For the pregnancy nausea, we would suggest an increase in the dosage
    to one half teaspoon in severe cases.
In most cases the one quarter teaspoon would be sufficient.
For those who are subject to the nausea and dizziness
    caused by the rocking motion,
we recommend ingestion one half hour
    before entering in to the rocking motion.
A sea sickness will necessitate one half teaspoon every half hour.
The patient may ingest up to a tablespoon per hour if necessary.

336 Placing the dried leaves of the apple blossom within a creamed lotion
    will enhance the healing properties of the cream
        for those who experience extreme dryness of the flesh.

Whether the dryness is due to a disease or to weather
>   or lack of balance within the inners, it will assist.

You will use one teaspoon to one half cup of cream.
It enhances any healing properties within the lotion.
If there is no lotion available place the leaves as given
>   within one quarter cup water, allow to sit for one half day,
>   and then place that upon the skin, and you will find it is beneficial.

337   You will understand that emotions are filtered
>   through all the bodily organs,
>   and they are aligned with the emotions of being.

Unexpressed anger will be felt within the bladder area.
It will manifest itself as a problem of urination.
When anger is withheld from expression over a long period of time,
>   a bladder infection will result.

The emotion of sorrow held within as grief
>   will manifest itself within the heart area.

As it is held within,
>   over time it begins to affect the arteries and they become plugged.

It is, Souls of earth, not conducive to wellness and good health
>   to withhold emotions.

They must be expressed,
>   and by expressed we are not in any way condoning
>   any vituperative actions upon another or upon self.

Recognize, emotions are part and parcel of being human,
>   but they are not meant to be any other than a lesson,
>   an opportunity to learn.

And by withholding self from the lesson,
>   you bring upon thy being a disease,
>   which must manifest itself in the physical manner.

For those who repress the emotions of love,
>   indeed, fear of love is a repression of love;
>   these will have problems with the lungs, unable in many cases,
>   when held for a number of years, to breathe correctly.

The fear of love held within and not released,
>   will over time lead to a deterioration of the lungs.

Hence, many diseases that baffle scientists and medical personnel,
>   and they need only look to the whole person, not just the physicality.

For those who repress the emotions of arrogance,
>   they will experience headaches.

Headaches are an indication to the being
>   that arrogance has taken over their relationships,
>   not only with others, but with self.

Those beings who have difficulty expressing any part of their being,
>   who have difficulty in relating their opinion even unto another,
>   who fear any sort of interaction,
>   who socially feel as an outcast from the world,
>   will experience difficulties within the colonic area
>   ranging from the diarrhea to the constipation,
>   and if not overcome, on into various diseases of the colon area.

It is imperative, Souls of earth, that you understand
>   the interrelationship of the body to emotions.

And understand the repression of emotions,
>   the refusal to overcome emotions that are detrimental to the being,
>   results with illness and disease.

338 We would ask you, Soul, to do this regularly
>   each day to maintain the balance of your Energy.

Place yourself at a table.
Join together the forefingers and the thumbs.
Place downward the palms on the table.
The big toes of either foot are placed together.
And then, Soul, we would have you straighten your spine,
>   look upward at a forty five degree angle.

Bring in from your aura, White Light.
We would have it, Soul, flood your being.
We would have you watch as it floods your being
>   from the top above your head, down to your toes.

You will understand, it will bring a balance to your system,
>   so that you will feel after the five minutes tingling all over.

And this is as it should be.
At the end of the five minutes, you will move your shoulders,
>   while holding in position, one, two, three, four, five, six.

And then you will feel the tingling on both sides,
>   and you have finished for that day.

339 Once every hour that you sit,
>   we would ask that you cross your ankles,
>   hold for the count of three,
>   wiggle your feet for a few seconds and then uncross.

Thrice do this each hour.
It will move the blood.

340   The inner portion of the apple blossom
        is most efficacious for the calming of a fevered brow.
Take and rub between your fingers and thumb
        the inner portion of the apple blossom
        and place this powdery substance
        across the brow of the fevered being.
Gently rub it in.
Both the aroma and the slight bit of oil that comes through
        will assist the being.

341   To assist in calming down the very high fevers,
        a sliver of the roots of the wallflower will do.
The sliver needs to be no larger than that thinness
        of two small sewing needles.
The inner part is that which you will place between the eyes,
        on the forehead, above the bridge of the nose,
Hold it in place for no more than ten seconds,
        and allow the inner portion to absorb some of the heat.
Remove it, wait three seconds, return it.
You may do this with the same sliver a maximum of five times.

342   We will speak on the properties of steam
        and its effect upon the human body.
When you have a quart of boiling water
        and you place within three drops vanilla,
        this will calm the fevered patient, the fevered child.
Allow the room to be a small one wherein the steam may escape
        near the patient and waft the odor unto the being's consciousness.
You will find the restlessness subsiding.

343   The leaves of the daffodil may be kept as dried
        as long as the drying is not done within a microwave.
It is preferable, in order to keep the properties intact, that it is air dried
        and allowed to naturally become a desiccated powder.
One quarter teaspoon for adults,
        one eighth teaspoon for children,
        mixed with a tinge of honey,

taken orally on a persistent basis, will cease all colds,
    all ailments affecting extremities of the body.
Hence those who have a nerve damage, as diabetic, will benefit.
We would recommend one dosage per day until recovery.
During what you term flu season in North America,
    it would be efficacious to ingest the dosage once per week.

344 We would speak of laughter, of healing and laughter.
Revitalize your being.
Laugh for the pure joy of life.
The laughter, Soul, is within.
Bring it forth, laugh, laugh the belly, laugh the belly.
That's why you have the representation of the Laughing Buddha,
    for he understood the healing power of laughter.
He understood the joy that sings through your being physically,
    with laughter.
He understood the cells vibrating to laughter.
Souls of earth, three minutes of day would resolve so many illnesses,
    so many tendencies to depression, to sadness, to sorrow.
You have this ability, this capability.

345 We would teach the properties of phlox.
All parts of the phlox have capabilities to assist mankind,
    from the roots to the stem, to the leaves to the flower,
    and to the inner portion of the phlox.
The inner stem of the petal of the flower, as minute as it is,
    has a powerful ability to assist in the sores resulting from herpes.
That minute, placed in one teaspoon of water, warmed, not hot,
    for hot will alleviate and enervate the power of the potion.
And so, warmed in a teaspoon of water with one drop of olive oil,
    and then placed directly upon by the eruptions
    caused by the herpes virus.
This will soothe any burning or soreness and applied daily
    will eventually heal the eruption.

346 We would have you know
    that the petals of the fireweed may be boiled as a tea.
Should fire not be available to boil water, place them
    in a glass container in the sun for four hours.
And you will have the same efficacy as with the boiled water.

We would suggest five fresh petals per cup.
For winter usage, you may dry the petals for tea,
    and that will require ten petals, instead of five fresh.
This tea will be most efficacious
    for those who are fighting infections.
The tea is to be sipped continuously throughout the day.
Two cups of tea for three days will be sufficient for a severe infection,
    longer for one that is difficult to remove because of complications.

347   The frangipani flower is most efficacious when dried,
    for in drying it becomes concentrated.
The fresh does not have as much efficacy,
    in this particular case, as the dried.
Once it is dried, grind it into a fine powder.
The frangipani powder may also be used to bring down
    swelling, inflammations, whether they be through bacteria
    or through stress, strains.
In this case you will use one half teaspoon powder
    to one tablespoon olive oil
    and you will make a poultice and place it upon the affected area.
Warmth is best, Soul.
If there is no cloth available,
    use the palm of your hand to hold it in place.
In the case of strains, the inflammation, you will again apply,
    for thirty minutes as often as is necessary,
    until the swelling, the inflammation has receded.

348   The branch of the pine scraped, dried and ground
    into fine powder will assist in overcoming any type of influenza.
The pine bark in powder form may be taken upon a cereal or a bread,
    but it is not to be heated.
You may place it in honey, again not heated.
In the most severe case of influenza,
    you would use one half teaspoon of the pine bark.
In lesser cases, one eighth teaspoon will suffice.

349   For those who have access to the baobab and are bitten,
    stung by insect,
        pluck a leaf and get it warm in your hand

and then place it upon the area of the sting with a bandage,
for it needs to be held in place for a period of a hour or less.
As soon as the pain has receded and the swelling has gone down,
it may be removed.
In order to stimulate the system to reject the toxin,
you must take two centimeters of the tip of the leaf,
and place that underneath the tongue,
for three minutes.

350 Ten leaves of the strawberry placed within a half cup of water,
allowed to sit in the sun for a period of three days,
and then you may strain the leaves out of the water
and use the water for those who have leprosy.
The placing of this water upon their being is most efficacious.

351 The petals of the deep purple clematis may be dried
and they may form a powdery substance after they are dried;
grind them up to form the powder.
The clematis powder mixed with one quarter cup of olive oil
to one tablespoon of powder is most efficacious for those
who have numbness in their feet or their hands.
Applied in the evening before retirement
and a cloth placed over the application
and then removed in the morning upon arising,
will assist in regaining the sense; the nerves will rejuvenate.
This is to be done daily until you begin to feel again
and the numbness has receded.
It is an imperative part of the process that these limbs be covered,
and hold the concoction within.
It is because the heat of the bindings will stimulate
the absorption within the flesh.
It would be most efficacious to do so as a preventative
before the digits are lost.
And, Soul, once leprosy has been in its early diagnosis;
if this treatment was to start early it would indeed
save many the use of their limbs.

352 The stem of the phlox when broken up into pieces
of less than one centimeter, dried, crushed,

and then boiled for one minute,
> draining the liquid from the boiling, will give you a skin tonic especially efficacious for the victims of leprosy.

It is to be placed gently upon the facial neck area,
> upon the eruptions on other parts of the body.

It is allowed to dry.
It is not to be wiped off or washed off for a period of three hours.
This is to be done three times daily until the eruptions begin to heal.
And then it will be done twice daily until you see the next level of healing,
> and then once daily until it is healed completely.

Also the ingestion of one tablespoon of this liquid daily for adults
> and one teaspoon for those under the age of thirteen
> afflicted with the leprosy,
> will assist the immune system to become strong and balanced.

353 The green tea after removal of the leaves,
> is efficacious for victims of leprosy.

In the making of the tea,
> use two tablespoons of green tea to one cup of water.

The tea is not to be boiled.
It is to be set within hot almost boiling water,
> and allowed to sit for ten minutes.

At the end of the ten minutes, remove the leaves
> and place the liquid upon the body.

Used as a wash, it is soothing.
As it enters into the pores, it provides a relief.
It will also impede the eating away of the flesh.
Soak the feet, the hands, the fingers, three times daily
> within the liquid of the green tea.

354 Lymphatic system exercise.
Soul, we would instruct.

Step 1
Place yourself upon a chair with a table.

Step 2
Place together the two forefingers and the thumbs,
> and hold them six inches above the table.

Step 3
You will then move your shoulders side to side, five times each side.

Step 4
At the end of the tenth, bring the fingers and the thumb
    unto the breastbone and gently press in to a count of five.
You will feel in the beginning a soreness, a tenderness.
As you continue with the exercise, you will notice that soreness,
    tenderness will disappear.

Step 5
Bring your arms outward again, all the way to the side, slowly,
    and you will hold for a count of five,
    and bring them back in again,
    perpendicular again, to the breastbone.
Press lightly, hold for a count of five.

Step 6
Move the arms straight out forward
    and fold the hands together, fingers intertwined.
Thumbs not folded, straight forward.
Hold for a count of five.

Step 7
Place together the two forefingers and the thumbs,
    and bring your hands to the sides just below the ear.
Press lightly, Soul, and hold for a count of ten.

Step 8
At the end of the count of ten, keeping your fingers and thumbs together,
    you will bring them downward into the position of palms up.
Hold for a count of three,
    deep breath and you are finished.
We would recommend for three days, three times per day,
    and then for ten days once per day.

355 We would speak on massage.
You have upon your earth plane
    a great variety types of massage for the human body.

We would have you understand the necessity
> to work always in a clockwise direction.

This will keep the massage
> in tune with the internal workings of your body,
> the internal workings of the flow of your inners.

When the massage or rubbing is counterclockwise,
> it sets up an irritation within the nerves of the being.

And not just in the particular spot where it is counterclockwise,
> but that irritation floods throughout,
> although most felt at the initial point of pressure.

And we would have you understand the flat of your hand,
> the palm of your hand is most efficacious for a massage.

This allows a greater area to be covered by the circular clockwise action.

The use of the fingertips is most efficacious
> when used as if you were playing a piano,
> not in circular motion clockwise or counterclockwise.

When using the fingers always
> as if you were moving across the piano, not rubbing,
> rubbing only to be done with the flat of the hand.

The two, whether the fingers or the palm,
> provide very different effects upon the body.

The use of the fingers as if you were playing a piano
> is most efficacious for those injuries caused by strains of the muscles.

It matters not where upon the body, even the ankles will be assisted.

When you are using your fingertips
> do not pound the 'keys', a slight pressure is sufficient.

When you are using the flat of your hand for deep tissue injury or tendons,
> for the arthritic ache, the pressure is to be light enough
> > that the being feels the circular motion
> > but not enough to cause pain.

When pain is felt,
> then ease the amount of pressure being applied in a circular motion.

There are times when the knuckles of the hand will be most efficacious.

And again this is to be done lightly.

You do not need to apply a great deal of pressure.

And you will know if you are applying too much pressure if there is pain
> and then you will ease up.

The knuckles may be most efficacious when placed
> upon either side of the spine and moved back and forth
> all the way down the spine.

Always starting at the very top of the neck and then moving downward,
>   one side and then the other side.
Even though there may only be pain on one side,
>   both sides always, Soul, for balance.
In all cases as a general rule of thumb, olive oil is most efficacious
>   and penetrates the skin as a preventative.
You may also understand that for strains and sprains
>   one drop oil of bergamot to two tablespoons olive oil applied lightly,
>   very gently will help to penetrate the massage.
For the deeper tissue injuries, we would suggest one drop oil of bergamot,
>   two drops eucalyptus in three tablespoons olive oil
>   and again applied lightly and gently.
For those afflicted with the rheumatoid arthritic pains
>   or arthritic pains of any kind, we would suggest one drop oil
>   of pure peppermint to one tablespoon olive oil applied lightly
>   and massaged in.

356 We speak with you on the properties of cinnamon.
And we speak of the outer bark, not the inner bark,
>   for the two are different in properties.
Grind extremely fine, almost to a powder;
>   the coarseness will not release the properties.
To assist in the healing of those afflicted with menopausal symptoms
>   of mood swings and temperature swings,
>   one eighth teaspoon ingested daily for a period of seven days
>   will be most efficacious to calm the symptoms.
Thereafter every other day, one eighth teaspoon
>   will persist in ameliorating the symptoms.
If you can only ascertain the inner bark, we suggest then you will need
>   three quarter teaspoon ground almost to powder form,
>   and this will alleviate.
For those who have completed the menopause,
>   and whose hormones are imbalanced,
>   we suggest one three quarter teaspoon of the cinnamon daily,
>   if it is the outer bark, it would be one eighth teaspoon.
We would ask that you not cook the cinnamon.
We would ask that it be placed in raw form upon food,
>   or in a water that has not been heated
>   or even in a juice that has not been heated.

Heating or cooking will kill the properties
> that will balance your hormones.

357 Those who have, who are afflicted
with diseases of the nervous system
will benefit from the application of the massage to the feet
three times daily and to the outer stomach area.
The application will be one fourth cup olive oil,
one drop rosemary, one drop geranium,
two drops lavender and one drop pure peppermint.
They will begin, shortly, to feel a lifting of the symptoms.

358 We speak of the properties of verbena.
Understand the healing properties of the verbena
are found in the majority in the roots.
When the plant flowers it is time to pull out the roots.
You must not pull out the complete plant.
Dig deeply around the plant and pull forth
only maximum three rootlings of each plant.
Re cover the rest of the plant for future growth.
Wash the soil from the root,
boil the roots and make a mash that becomes liquefied.
You will use the liquid in the curing of internal parasitic diseases.
It will flush from the system all parasites of any form.
Use only upon the human body.
A quarter teaspoon each day, four days,
is sufficient to cleanse the body of all parasites.
It is especially efficacious for those worms found within the body
in the Amazon region and in China.

359 We speak on the properties of barberry.
This plant is most efficacious for those diseases of the nervous system,
whether they be Parkinson
or even unto the very mild forms of tremors, of nervousness
as is commonly called a fright from the inside,
may also be helped by barberry.
The berries are to be plucked in the early morning;
directly after a sunrise they are at their peak of perfection.
They are then to be mashed, mushed into a liquidly pulp.

It is important that the skins remain on
> and that skins are crushed until they become a very soft pulp,
> for you will use both the pulp and the liquid.

The liquid is to be taken for those who have nervousness of character,
> one eighth teaspoon every three days for no more than twelve days.

Then rest for thirty four days before using again.
For those who have diseases of the nervous system such as the Parkinson,
> one teaspoon on the first day,
>> every three hours for a total of four teaspoons.

On the second day, three teaspoons every three hours,
> on the third day two teaspoons every three hours,
> on the fourth day unto the twelfth day, one teaspoon every day.

And then you will rest for the next thirty four days before resuming
> once daily one teaspoon until you have control of the tremors.

Soul, it is an alleviation.
For those afflicted with the severity of the disease,
> bathing the body with the pulp once daily for twelve days.
> in conjunction with the ingestion of the liquid will
> bring about an almost complete relief of all symptoms.

The combination of the pulp and the liquid are powerful.
When the pulp is placed upon the body
> it is to be placed upon the limbs.

It is not necessary to fully bathe the torso.
It is the limbs that we would have you massage in with the pulp.
And then allow the pulp to stay upon the skin
> for a period of fifteen minutes before washing.

360 The pink sedum is most efficacious
> for those beings who have lost a limb.

Who suffer from the phantom pain of the lost limb.
The pink, five florets, is to be air dried, mixed with olive oil,
> then placed directly upon the stump of the lost limb.

And bandaged thereto, to stay for at least for at least two hours.
This will alleviate the phantom pain.

361 For those experiencing pains here and there throughout body,
> we would suggest, imbibe cream of tartar,
>> one half teaspoon three mornings,
>> then abstain two mornings,
>> and then three mornings one half teaspoon.

We would request honey and lemon juice, one tablespoon honey
    to one half teaspoon lemon juice, to be taken every other day
        after the cream of tartar
        and continue the honey and lemon juice
        every other day for thirty days.
At the end of the thirty days, we would suggest the baking soda,
    one half teaspoon for five mornings,
    three mornings abstain,
    and five more mornings one half teaspoon baking soda.
This will, Soul, re balance body.

362 We would have you understand
    the effect of a music beat upon the body,
    in particular the health of the body.
The heartbeat, Soul, is no accident.
The tempo of the heartbeat in its highest form
    is most efficacious to bring about wellness to the body.
The mechanics of the beat of the heart
    go beyond the blood flow of the system.
Understand, Souls of earth, the natives of your earth plane
    use the heartbeat in many ceremonies.
It is healing.
It encourages wellness within your being.
The heartbeat tempo, the rhythm is also used
    in many of your music compositions
    and you will find those beneficial when overcoming an illness.
We would also have you understand that
    that beat may be placed upon the body.
Just above heart center
    place the thumb and the small finger together.
Your other three fingers held just immediately below your collar bone
    upon the left hand side.
Gently press into the flesh with the three fingers
    in the tempo of the heartbeat.
The heartbeat has a rhythm
    and you are copying that rhythm externally to your body
    to encourage healing, to encourage wellness.
If you encounter, Soul, pain or aching
    as you are copying the heartbeat rhythm,
    that is an indication of where the body requires healing.

If the pain is found in the area of the forefinger,
> the healing is required in the lower portion of your body.

If the pain is encountered in the second finger area
> then it is your torso that requires the healing.

If the pain, the soreness, is felt with the third finger
> then healing is required from your chin up, in the head area.

And you would then concentrate with the eye upon that area of the body.
So you are using the rhythm of the heart,
> using the tapping, the alerting of the body to the need for healing
> and you are using the eye to focus healing upon that area.

Triad, Soul.
This may be done periodically throughout your day.
There is no set limit or minimum amount of times
> that this technique may be used.

It is also a way to check out the wellness areas of your body.
Even if you do not feel any particular pain or illness,
> checking will indicate if there is
> an incipient pain or illness materializing.

And then you would know where to focus your healing.
If you feel no pain then you are in balance.
Using the technique of the heartbeat and feeling no pain or soreness
> as you press into the flesh, indicates
> wellness and also encourages peak performance of the body.

You will use the heartbeat rhythm
> of a healthy heart at rest in its tranquil state.

363 We have come forward to explain the benefits of posture.
The straight spine allows the fluid to freely do
> what it was meant to do.

The posture affects the whole body,
> especially the back, the neck, and the head.

Many of the aches and pains, many of the headaches,
> the shoulder, the neck aches experienced are due to the posture;
> the bent over, the spine not being straight, Soul.

Understand that even if the physical body has an impediment
> the mind may still inhabit the spine, inhabit straight
> so that the fluid permeates and flows freely as it was meant to do.

When the body is crimped, when the posture
> has the head bent over, the shoulders hunched,
> it interferes with the flow physically and mentally.

We would ask that you focus thrice daily on checking your posture.
This would be beneficial and most efficacious for all beings,
> to remind themselves of how they sit,
> of how they stand, of how they lay.

364 We would speak to you of sleep.
Upon your earth, sleep is known as a period of rest
> for the body and the mind.
But we would have you know
> sleep takes place upon three levels of awareness.
You have, Souls, your earth level
> and these are dreams that you may sometimes recall,
> these are dreams wherein you reenact your present life.
The second level of sleep contains dreams of past lives,
> of events that have bearing upon this lifetime.
They are a font of information and worthy of recording.
They are guided, as in a guided meditation.
The third level is when you ascend unto a teaching plane, Farside.
It is an opportunity given for Spirit to speak to Soul.
There are those Souls who can not reach a point of rest,
> of stillness, and therefore do not reach this level.
There are Souls whose sleep is interrupted
> by a physical condition or a mental worrisome aberration.
They do not attain this level.
Sleep is indeed, in more ways than one,
> a restoration of the energies of your being,
> for it does more than effect the body, the physical.
It affects the mind, the will and the Soul.
You may, beloved beings, Souls of earth,
> request a teaching night as you enter into slumber.
It is your guides who will give you the breath of teaching that is for you,
> and it is in the realm of your guides as to whether or not
> you will recall the teaching when you awake.
Some teachings are to be as yeast and allowed to leaven within the being,
> and not immediately recalled into the conscious state of earth.
Some teachings you may never intentionally be aware of.
And yet you will notice a differing attitude,
> a differing awareness of that which is about thee.
It is not only in a state of meditation
> that you have opportunity to be taught.

Indeed, many will find it difficult to ascertain
    the relationship from past to present.
You will know by the use of the eye.
You will know by the strangeness, by the lack of familiarity.
And yet there will be some similarity to your current life
    whether it is within your own pattern of actions,
        your own pattern of premises of thinking, of thought,
        or whether, indeed, it bears similarity to those other Souls
    with whom you interact.
A record will bring forth a pattern that is recognizable.

365 We would speak of sound and the importance of sound
    upon patients in the later stages of any disease.
It is the sound of all that is around the patient,
    the sounds are earth sounds.
For healing, the toning of the sound is of utmost importance.
The toning affects various parts of the body and the mind.
The healer must understand the importance of toning
    to that particular patient,
        for what is efficacious for one,
        may be only gently soothing to another.
It is imperative when the body is fighting the later stages of diseases
    that the discordant note is not sounded.

366 The elderberry wine, it is a tonic.
It is overall a tonic of well being for the elderly body.
We would recommend a glass daily upon the age seventy.
But we caution always the toxicity.
Beware the toxicity and know, Soul, from whence it came.

367 We would have you understand the necessity for water
    when recovering from an illness or injury.
Always when recuperating after the crisis has passed,
    increase the intake of water, for it helps to flush from the system
    the toxins that have accumulated through the injury or illness.
For each twenty five pounds of being, up to the age of thirteen,
    increase the intake of water by one half cup daily.
For the babe we would ask that you bathe,
    that you wipe down the child with a wet cloth often
    so that the pores absorb the water.

For those above the age of thirteen one cup more per day.
This is to continue even for one week
>after you believe you are completely recuperated.
For those areas who do not have access to fresh clean water,
>we ask that you place within the water,
>>pure spearmint leaves, dried, five tablespoons per quart.
After twenty four hours, you may filter out the leaves
>and drink the water.
If you have available only the oil of the pure spearmint,
>two drops to a quart of water.

Exercise
368 We would suggest the following routine to invigorate the body,
>to keep it toned, or for it to become toned.
For three minutes march in place,
>bring the knees up as far as you can.
You will find that if you can not bring them up very high
>in the very beginning,
>>that in time you will be astounded at how high you can raise them.
The movement is not to be done quick march.
It is to be done slow march, Souls, so that you focus upon your body,
>so that you focus upon the internal workings of the body,
>>that you are aware of the blood, the bone, the sinew, the muscles.
It is optimal for each leg to benefit for the full three minutes.
Then we would have you sit in a chair if you are not already,
>and place your being bending forward as far as you can.
Bring your hands down to grip the chair
>and hold that position for the count of three seconds.
And then slowly bring your being back up.
As you bring your being back up, you will inhale
>as far as you are able, so that your stomach touches the spine.
You will do this three times for the first week.
Then you will increase four times the next week.
And then, every week thereafter unto a maximum of ten.
As you are doing the bending exercise in the chair, focus on your body.
Focus on your digestive system,
>on the miracle that takes place within your being.
And then you will place your arms fully extended
>on either side of your being, palms up,
>>and bring your palms forward.

Hold that position to the count of seven seconds.
And then, Soul, you will bring your arms up
>   as far as you are able over the top of your head,
>   as high as you can extend your arms,
>   and hold that position for the count of seven.

Keep your head upright as far as you are able.
And then, Soul, bring your hands downward.
Extend your arms fully to either side and move your hands
>   so that the palms are now facing your back.

And hold that for the count of seven.
And then slowly bring them back in
>   to the resting position against your body.

The last exercise, Soul, is to simply sit and move your head
>   in the position of acquiescence twice, up and down, slowly.

If you become dizzy, stop, rest a moment and then proceed again.
And then we would ask that you stand and move
>   in a clockwise circle, slowly.

After you have completed the circle, take your arms
>   and place them in the hug position
>   and congratulate yourself and praise your body.

Deep breath and you have completed the exercise for the day.

369 We would have you glide as in a waltz, as in the step of a waltz.
Each day play a gentle waltz and move to the rhythm.
For your body, Soul, will connect to the cadence of the music.
Allow your arms to drift out.
Do not hold them in place.
Allow them also to glide with the music as your feet glide with the music,
>   as your body glides with the music.

And allow your mind to glide also.
Free it to move with the music.
We would have you do this daily.
This will invigorate and tone your being.
It will tone not only the flesh of your being but it will tone the mind,
>   for you will find it greatly relaxing.

In the midst of your busy schedule take time for this exercise.
This we say unto you.
Understand, Soul, it is all done in the cadence
>   and in the glide of the music, softly.

370   We would have you stand or sit against a wall.
Bring your arms to your side
>   and then slowly bring them out, palms down
>   and have the arms rise slowly
>   until they are at their utmost extension
>   and flat against the wall, with your palms out against the wall.

Take a deep breath, hold the deep breath for a count of six
>   and then slowly exhale for a count of seven.

Slowly bring the arms down.
When they reach the midpoint, the palms are to rest against your thighs.
Repeat this exercise thrice.
This will increase the circulation in your being.
It will also give you a moment to contemplate
>   away from the busyness.

371   We would have you, Soul, when you are engaged in a activity
>   for more than fifteen minutes straight,
>   whether it be exercise or bent over reading or on a machine,
>   take your right arm, bring it up
>   and place it on the back of the neck.

The palm of your hand will rest upon the back of your neck.
Then take the left and the left will rest over the right hand.
And then bring your elbows close to your ears.
And then out again, in and out, slowly thrice.
Deep breath.
And you will feel reinvigorated.

372   While at the computer each hour,
>   take and place the arms fully extended to either side of the body.

The palms facing toward the computer.
And then move the hands upward.
Touch the thumbs at the top of the head and then
>   slowly bring them down.

And do this thrice.
And then deep breath and whooooosh.

373   We would have you understand the importance of movement.
Far too often there is no movement for the human body,
>   that is considered exercise and it coagulates the blood.

Exercise daily is imperative to the wellbeing of a body.

When you sit in a chair for a period of time,
>   your body becomes internally stiffened.
We would have you, when you are going to be sitting
>   for any lengthy period of time,
>   and lengthy is more than fifteen minutes,
>   we would have you move your feet up and down.

Touch the floor, lift your feet up, touch the floor, lift your feet up.
You will do this in sequence, starting with the left and then your right.
Left and then the right.
Left and then the right.
And you will do this at least ten times every fifteen minutes,
>   in order to keep the optimum flow of the blood within your body.

The rhythm of the up and the down is not to be done quickly
>   but in a balanced cadence of your seconds,
>   one up, hold for three, one down, one up, hold for three, one down.

This will be especially helpful to those confined to a chair.
Soul, the bedridden, the unable to move
>   may be exercised through massage.

When you are caretakers for a being who is unable to leave a chair
>   or bed or move on their own, that would be the same rhythm;
>   move up and down, up, hold for three, down; up, hold for three, down.

In the case where the beings are bedridden this is imperative
>   to be done once an hour for healing.

It will stimulate the body to heal.

374 Focus on relaxing the body.
Stand at the bottom of steps.
Both feet together.
Arms at the side, straight down.
Relax the shoulders and step up to the first step, left leg first.
And then bring it back down.
And then bring the other one up to the first step and bring it back down.
And then walk up the steps slowly and focus on the body.

375 We ask that you place feet daily at the bottom of the stairs,
>   hold to the railing, Soul.

Move your right foot onto the first step.
Hold it for the count of three and bring it down.
And then the same with your left, to the count of three and bring it down.

Repeat five times in a row.
Hold your body straight, your head upright,
> your back as straight as you can while doing these
> and you will find less ache of the hip.

376 You have, Souls of earth, marching.
We have found that this is most efficacious for the heart.
It stimulates not only the heart but all your inners
> in addition to toning the muscles.

Where possible vigorous marching at the rate of
> seven minutes continuous marching,
> is most efficacious for the general toning
> of the whole body.

You need not march around.
You may march in place.
But it is important that the marching not be done
> stomping the feet.

You do not want to jar your system only invigorate it.
And so you march up and down as pistons, but gently.

377 This will provide a tension release to your whole being top to toe.
You will find yourself 'haaaah!' after the exercise, for you will feel better.
This, Soul, is because of the sitting that often is required of your body.
This will bring circulation into the arms and into the back.
Often we would have you do this:

Step 1
Massaging of the whole hands, back and palm five times,
> as if you were wiping your hands.

Step 2
Place the fingers intertwined, the thumbs up
> and we would have you move five times back and forth.

Step 3
Reverse the hands, palms out, fingers intertwined
> and push your arms out, keeping your back straight for five seconds.

Step 4
Turn the hands toward you and release.

Step 5
Place your feet where your soles touch each other as you sit.
It does not require the whole sole to touch the whole sole,
     as long as there is a portion touching.

Step 6
Straighten your spine, hands on a surface.
Hold that position for ten seconds,
     allowing the tension to drain from your being.
Starting from the top of your head all the way down to the tips of your toes.

Step 7
Deep breath through the nostrils, hold for three seconds,
     and breathe out gently through the mouth for the count of five.
And then, release the feet.

378 We would have you take five minutes thrice daily
     to rejuvenate your being.
Put your hands palm up upon a surface,
     touching the left over the right.
Close your eyes,
     placing your head down.
And simply breathe in to the count of three,
     breathe out to the count of four.
You will do this breathing, Soul, not continuously,
     but you will do it thrice within the five minutes.
The rest of the time maintain your normal breathing pattern.
At the end of the five minutes, place your hands behind your neck,
     press into the indentation at the back of the neck,
     where the skull ends and hold that for two seconds.
And you will find yourself relaxed and able to carry on.

379 Exercise! Exercise! Exercise!
Walking.
Indeed, Soul, until you exercise you will not understand the very basic
     difference it will make in your being, not only physically
     but in the spirit of your human self, the spirit of your Soul.
It affects more than the physical.
We would ask you to try for three weeks.
And then, make your choice to either continue or to cease.

It must be the sustained walking, whether it is ten minutes here
      or five minutes there; up to the thirty minutes per day.
Even if you walked in the house,
      it is to be a continuous for those five or ten minutes.
We would have you understand the lactic acid in your muscles
      is assisted to regain its balance by the exercise.
And you have now the reason for the movement required.
You will find yourself invigorated
      to the point where you will automatically
           increase on your own to a further few minutes.
Your body and mind will be synchronized, Soul,
      and you will experience great joy.
For it has more than one benefit to your body.
It increases the flow within your body.
It brings richer blood to the mind.
You have a clarity, Soul, that will occur.
And you will find your relaxing moments
      of greater benefit for this exercise.

380 Souls, loping is a method of walking.
A lope is most efficacious for those beings
      who are in prime physical condition but who are incredibly stressed.
A loping run for ten minutes will bring the stress level down
      and will also indeed, reduce the blood pressure
           bringing soothing surceases to the troubled being.

Food

381 As in all cases of foods manufactured upon your earth,
      we would ask that you purify as much as possible
           before the ingestion into your being.
We would ask that you peruse all labels
      and choose that which has the most wellness giving,
           which has the least, preferably none, manmade additives.
Additives such as even artificial flavoring have an effect upon the body,
      for they are not natural.
Any synthetic, Souls, may not necessarily exacerbate the body,
      but will, indeed, have no use to the body.
All within the earth has become toxic to an extent.
And so the body is an incredible production
      in its ability to strain toxins, to filter toxins;

      but, Souls of earth, the bodies are becoming overwhelmed
      and require purified before entering in.

382   Souls of earth, your planet is afflicted
      and increasingly with diseases such as Alzheimer.
And you will find they are not strictly for the aged, the very aged.
They will become increasingly common for younger beings
      due to the style of eating.
The lack of nutrients is of great contributor to Alzheimer.
Souls of earth, much of your food has leached through your toxins
      the majority of its nutrients.
And many will pay the penalty.
We would urge all mankind to eat to live, to nurture their beings,
      to nurture the beings of the children,
      to understand the need for balance in all things, including food.

383   The amaranth may be used as a pick me up.
Four leaves placed within a salad or upon a meal, upon any food.
Not cooked, indeed not, for cooking will destroy the efficacity.

384   To bring about a balance of chi
      we need you to understand the process would be long and involved.
This we tell you, Soul, not to discourage but to have you clearly understand
      that once embarked upon the process it must come to fruition
      only with all the parameters given.
To begin with, avoid all sugar from the diet
      with the exception of one tablespoon honey, daily,
      and one fruit in the vitamin C category, daily.
All other sugars are to be forbidden.
Refrain from additional salt to food,
      no salt within the cooking, no salt after the cooking.
No processed foods.
You have available to you herbs, hundreds of herbs,
      that will give flavor to your food
      and there is within certain foods a nominal amount of salt.
This regime along with the others we will give,
      must be over a six months period.
Thereafter a moderation will be called for in all ingestion of foods.
During the six months, daily oatmeal, a half cup in some form
      not necessary in one meal; it may be spread throughout the day.

One half teaspoon cinnamon per day.
You may also have one teaspoon currants daily.
Refrain from red or pink meat for the six months.
Fowl and fish are acceptable with the exception of the salted fish,
    either by the processor or by the fish itself.
Additionally, you must undertake exercise.
The mind is sluggish.
The body is sluggish.
Even, Soul, if you were simply to march in place
    and piston your arms daily ten minutes,
        you would begin to be rejuvenated and it will assist in the balance.
All vegetables are permissible.
Beans are permissible but not canned, for often salt is added.
Rice is permissible as is your pasta but not in wheat form.
All wheat is to be excluded for the six months.
And you will begin this regimen with the cleansing of the body:
    three days one quarter teaspoon cream of tartar in water or juice,
    two days no cream of tartar,
    and then complete with
        four days one quarter teaspoon cream of tartar.
You will then wait three days and begin a seven day baking soda.
One quarter teaspoon per day, five days, one day none, and one day resume.
We would also suggest the ingestion of vitamin E,
    preferably from a natural source, not manufactured,
        to the limit of eight hundred milligrams per day.
We would also suggest
    one evening of primrose oil capsule per day of one thousand.
Additionally, Soul, you will ingest vitamin A and D combination.
Not separate,
    combination of five thousand vitamin A, four hundred vitamin D.
As you begin to feel more in balance with your being,
    we would ask that you increase from ten minutes per day of activity
        gradually increasing up to thirty minutes per day of vigorous exercise.
By vigorous we mean the pumping of the arms and legs.
You need not run, you need not jog,
    you may do this standing in place,
        although you may add other forms of exercise, Soul.
And we would have you each morning perform the east ritual
    and sit after the ritual for fifteen minutes
        in quiet contemplation of colors of healing.

385 We would bring to you today knowledge
      of the effects of caffeine upon the human body.
We would have you understand caffeine is a stimulus
     and as such works upon the nerves of your being
     and when the nerves are over stimulated,
     then all manner of complications arise,
     as the body is jolted out of its calmness by the caffeine.
Your hands may not shake,
     but your inners are jittery and shaking.
Your heart is being over stimulated constantly.
And so we would ask you to reconsider the dependency upon caffeine.

386 In all cases of cancer the papaya is the closest to an efficacious food.
The pulp of the papaya has an erroneous effect upon the cancer growth.
It fools the cancer cells and retards the progress.
But, Soul, the dosage depends upon the variables involved.
For example, a patient with the growth of a nodule
     the size of a thumbnail would only require
     two medium papaya per day.
The patient who has the cancer metastasized
     and tumors larger than the thumbnail,
     would require six to ten papaya.
It is the pulp that holds the efficacity, not so much the juice.
Soul, we require a slight warming to room temperature, not cooked,
     for that would destroy the enzymes.
Although it is the pulp that has the most efficaciousness,
     there is a generality connected with the juice
     that makes the chemical reaction efficacious.
We would also suggest the warm bath three times per day
     and the rubbing gently, massaging into the flesh the olive oil.
No vigorous rubbing, the application must be done gently but thoroughly
It has two prongs; the olive oil will interact with the papaya
     in a most efficacious manner.
And the application itself of the oil will soothe the patient,
     and so it reacts even more so with the soothing,
     for the flesh is under attack.
We would recommend, if anything is used in combination
     with the olive oil, that it be geranium oil.
Light, light, for the flesh needs the mind to be calm.

When chemotherapy has been undertaken
> to fight against cancerous growth,
>> it is imperative that copious amounts of water are ingested each day.

No less than ten glasses per day; ideally, sixteen.

It is imperative that these toxins are cleansed from the body
> as soon as possible.

And it is imperative that the patient refrain
> from salt intake during the treatment.

We suggest no salt intake a minimum of five days
> before the treatment and a minimum of ten days after.

387 We would have the being understand the Crohn's
> exacerbated greatly by the food intake.

The being is excessive in intake of sugar.

The being is excessive in intake of acidities.

The being needs to refrain from all beef and pork
> for a three month period
>> in order to bring the total body back into balance.

Thereafter in a moderate amount
> the being may return to the ingestion of that flesh.

We would suggest to refrain from any flour,
> with the exception of the oat flour.

The being requires a full rest of the digestive system.

And in that vein, we would suggest for three months no dairy products
> brought about from the cow.

After the three months, the being may return
> but again in a moderate balanced diet.

The being is almost totally alkaline
> and needs to bring the body into wellness.

We would also suggest the refraining from caffeine.
> for the three month period.

The caffeine whether it is from your fizz in a diet drink,
> or coffee or tea is irritating to the inners.

We would ask the being for three months
> to refrain from any type of inhalation of smoke, any type.

We would also ask the being in its plan of wellness achievement
> to meditate fifteen minutes, three times daily
>> for the three month period.

And it will bring about an attitudinal shift that will be most efficacious.

388 We would draw your attention to the necessity
of purifying areas of disaster.
For if they are not purified the effects linger year after year.
Think you the waters are contained only within the area of a disaster?
Indeed not, that water enters everywhere.
One drop from the Arctic Circle enters in to all of earth.
A drop from any point on earth
enters in to all of the waters in the land of earth.
Souls of earth, it is imperative you understand
this basic concept of wellness, of health.
Bring forth your energies and purify all areas of disaster.
And we have recommendations for those areas of disaster.
Salt is a great leavener.
To gain water in times of crisis; salt,
boiled for twenty three minutes minimum,
will neutralize most toxins
enough for the beings to live upon, to survive.
This needs be a table salt.
The ratio is three tablespoons to three quarts.

389 The juniper may also be boiled as a tea.
Taking the juniper berries of this bush,
six berries placed in boiled water
and allowed to steep for three minutes,
produces what you call a tisane
that is soothing to a being who is in grief, who is in shock.
These berries whether dried or fresh
would be most efficacious as part of an emergency kit
for any disaster.
Brew pots and pots, Souls, and give unto the victims.
Each cup, with the berries sifted out, will be as a balm
to the spirit and to the body of the victim.
The berries themselves are not to be ingested,
merely the tea made from the berries.
The berries are not, even in their dried state to be crushed,
only thrown into the water.

390 We speak on the properties of garlic.
Garlic is beneficial and efficacious
in the warding off of what you call flu.

Indeed your ancient myths had a grain of truth
    when they said that garlic would ward off vampire.
For does not the flu drain from you your energy!
Garlic in many respects responds in the same vein as olive oil.
It is a preventative.
It acts as an emollient within your system.
Most important it enhances the immune system of your being.
We speak not of cooked garlic.
At the most we suggest simply a slight warming of the garlic,
    oft times, in a bit of olive oil
        for the combination enhances each other.
When the garlic is cooked it loses some of the potency for protection.
It is the raw garlic that is most efficacious.
We would suggest you may chew or you may mash
    one quarter teaspoon for adult
    and one sixteenth teaspoon for child below twelve.
This may be placed within another food that is cool, not within a hot food.

391 We would also have the understanding
    the properties of raw garlic are most efficacious
    in building the blood,
        when it has become anemic due to any type of illness.
One quarter teaspoon for adults and one sixteenth for child below twelve,
    used twice daily for a period of thirteen days,
        will bring the blood back unto its original potency.
Any deficiency due to illness that is in the blood
    will be brought back into balance.
Garlic enhances the immune system, balances the blood.
It is not, Soul, a thinner, in the amounts we have given.

392 How to grow ginseng.
Where possible it would behoove the planter,
    the sower of the seed to gain pure seed.
Ideally, it is placed within a sheltered area where the sun may shine
    only part of the day, so that it faces east
    and then there is shelter as the sun moves around.
It would also be efficacious to place a small shelter
    for the first ten days of germination.

The shelter may be of paper,
> for ginseng requires gentleness in all handling.

Do not place manure within the plant.
Do not place within the plant bones.
A pine bark, a small sliver of pine bark
> will cause the growth of a healthy plant.

The sliver need not be beyond two inches
> by one inch of measurement.

This is all the fertilizer it requires.

393 We would speak upon itching,
> that itching that has no discernible cause but often times,
> even without seeing an eczema or psoriasis or a rash,
> a being will itch unbearably.

This is, Soul, from an internal problem, not from the skin itself
> but it is an eruption which may be caused by a variety.

To relieve, you would mix a cleanser: one quarter cup olive oil,
> one teaspoon rosemary, ground fine,
> add to this one drop rosemary oil, one drop geranium oil,
> and one drop bergamot oil.

And place upon the itching wherever it may be.
While the itching is attacking your being
> we would have you daily ingest one tablespoon of oat bran.

We would also request that you daily manage to ingest
> one quarter teaspoon of rosemary ground
> and one quarter teaspoon olive oil until the itching subsides.

These may be mixed or placed upon food but not cooked.

394 We would discuss with you the detrimental properties
> of that which you call lettuce.

Understand, Souls, all was placed within your world,
> within the earth plane, for the benefit of mankind.

It is pure in its being, in its offering to Creator
> to enter in to be used by mankind for wellness,
> for sustenance of being.

And mankind refutes this gift with its particular
> need to alter that which was given, with its need to experiment
> to gain in greed more from the plant than was offered.

Your geneticists are altering to the detriment of mankind
    that which was given in Purity.
We would have you know there are very few minimal pockets left
    where the planting, the raising, the care,
    the feeding of the lettuce is done in purity, in goodness.
You have before you on your tables
    alterations which do little to nourish and feed the flesh of your body.
We would have you know that it is a detrimental to your being
    to ingest these altered particles of being.
We would recommend that you not ingest any with the exception
    of those seedlings that are pure in being
    and that you know have been raised, nurtured
    and cared for without pesticide.
We would have you understand the pesticides used by mankind today,
    genetically affect your children in a detrimental manner.
The effects will not be recognized fully by mankind for generations,
    but they will trace back to the alteration of the present day.
For that which will be, the effects of the ingestion of today,
    that will be carried within the womb of the females
    will cause suppurating sores to erupt upon the newborn.
Upon the newborn!
Within the womb it will begin.
We ask that you alter now the pain of the future.

395 We would speak to you of your cupboards.
Within each cupboard we have for you a primary items:
    a mortar and pestle able to contain at least
    one quarter cup of ingredients;
    a syringe, it may hold a teaspoon of liquid;
    a glass bowl for mixing at least two cups.
Dried oregano, dried rosemary, dried basil, dried thyme,
    and dried cardamom,
    all within glass containers with tightly sealed lids,
    this will assist in dryness, in storage capacity, length.
A small packet of dried mustard,
    a container of vinegar, white,
    a container of vinegar, cider.
It is also ideal to have on hand oil of rosemary,
    oil of lavender and oil of geranium.

We would also suggest that you have on hand chamomile in dried form,
> in glass containers.

These will, Soul, comprise your basic medicine chest.

It is not to say that there are others that will be used from time to time.

396 We would have you understand that the pine bark,
> boiled to a mush, although stringy, will be palatable.

Take a piece of the pine bark no more than three inches by three inches,
> scrape the outer edge of the bark.

The inner part of the bark is that which we would have you boil
> until it becomes soft and able to be eaten.

The saliva will help draw out the nourishment of the bark.

And you need only, Soul, a small marble sized piece to chew
> and it will help give stamina to the body.

It will provide nourishment in times of dire need.

For the young babe or the elderly without teeth,
> mash and grind it until they may enter it in.

If available, add peppermint leaves to help with the taste.

Once it has been boiled, the concoction
> may be saved for further use and allowed to cool.

One cup of water of the water used to boil the inner bark,
> three times a day will assist any being to ward off malnutrition.

The young child up to seven years of age
> will require only half a cup three times a day.

Once it has been boiled, the concoction
> may be saved for further use and allowed to cool.

It is not necessary to drink it hot.

397 We would have you understand beetles.

Beetles, Souls of earth, are prevalent throughout the earth.

The bark of the beetles, their shell,
> can be used to provide a manner of protein.

The beetle must be more than three centimeters in length
> to provide any nourishment.

The size is important,
> for anything less does not have the concentration of protein.

The shell is placed within hot water, but not boiling,
> and allowed to become malleable, softened.

If there is no heating available,
> the water must be placed in the sun to warm up.

As it becomes malleable, you will know
> that the protein is being leached, entering in to the water.

As soon as it is softened to the point where it begins
> to break apart if it is rubbed, then it is at prime moment.

You may strain the shells from the water and the water may be ingested.
You may then take the shells that you have strained
> and dry them, grind them to a fine powder.

And this may be mixed with any water and ingested.
There needs to be no more than one half cup of water for every three shells,
> that will provide at least ten percent
> of your daily protein requirement.

And at times of famine, this will be most efficacious.

Color Healing

398   Beloved Souls, we would speak upon and delineate for you,
> the properties of crystal.

Crystalline structures willingly placed upon the earth,
> crystalline structures willingly giving of their being
> to enhance and to enable mankind to pursue its purpose, its goal.

Each crystalline being has within it color.
Each color designated for purpose of healing emotional instabilities.
The color, the shades of yellow, have as their purpose clarity of mind,
> dispensing the opaqueness that causes instability,
> that causes confusion, within the cortex of the brain.

The clear crystalline yellow of citrine is a valuable ally in this respect
> but all yellows are valued for this.

To enhance clarity of mind and the purpose,
> hold in the open palm of the right hand,
> a crystal of yellow color and its companion crystal of a blue shade.

Bring both open palms and crystals forward in front of the third eye
> and request clarity of mind.

You will hold thus for no less than twenty eight seconds
> and as long as you desire.

The blue shades of crystals are enhancers to all other crystal formations.
They increase the power of all other crystalline formations.
In all cases, when using crystals to heal, mentally or physically,
> you will always have a blue crystal in the left hand

and depending upon the problem,
varying color of crystals in the right hand.
There is no enhancement required
for the crystalline being in its natural state.
It does not enhance the power of the crystal to abrade it,
to scrape it, to polish it, to shape it.
These are enhancements given by mankind,
which to some increases the beauty of the object,
but does not increase the power of the object.
We would have you know it is unnecessary but acceptable.
The minute crystal, the size of your fingernail,
has not less power or ability to enhance
than the crystal that fills your palm.

399 Amber, ancient amber, Souls of earth,
botanicals or insects caught within the amber
will not affect its properties.
Amber when held within the palms of both hands
even though it is in itself light in weight
will become heavy as it begins its work.
Amber is most efficacious when attempting to overcome
disability of the mind, any disability of the mind,
whether it be of a learning disability
or whether it be a tendency to mental illness.
The size of the amber is not of importance.
What is of importance is that the amber is cleansed before use.
Cleansing is to be done with one half teaspoon of sea salt
or salt to one half cup of drinking water.
The amber is placed within and allowed to sit within the sun
for three minutes.
And then place the stone within your hands palms up,
close one palm over the other, and gently roll the stone,
first right over left palm, next left over right palm,
always moving clockwise direction.
After you have warmed the stone, with your hand palm up
hold so that your fingertips touch
the stone in the center of your palm.
And then relax your being
and close the fingers over the stone.

Bring your closed hand unto the solar plexus.
Place both hands against the body and hold for three minutes.
Deep breath, open the palms of your hands
    and place the stone within your hands palms up.
Close one palm over the other and gently roll the stone,
    first right over left palm, next left over right palm,
    always moving clockwise direction.

400   Souls of earth, we would speak of blackness.
We would speak of the comfort
    and the warmth enveloped within blackness.
Much of humanity equates blackness to evil, with impurity, with disdain.
Blackness, indeed the color of black, has a great spectrum of shades of color.
Each of the shades of color have a meaning,
    have relevance to your being, to your growth.
They also have relevance as do all things upon the earth
    to their placement within your life.
There are no coincidences,
    this you have been taught many time by our revered teachers.
And indeed, there are none.
When a color comes into your life in any form, it is an indication
    that you should pay particular attention to the shade.
The shade of a black that is almost a blue,
    has to do with and has an affinity for a spirituality.
When you touch upon such a color of the earth,
    when you are attracted to such a color,
    when you wish for clothes of attire of this color, or a painting of,
    it is your Soul mirror to you,
    calling attention to your placement,
    in that particular time of your life, of spirituality.
And, Souls of earth, when you are attracted to this particular shade
    in more than one instance, it is a time to look upon
    the placement of spirituality within your life.
Does it have placement way, way, way down your list
    or is it placed in importance at the top of your list?
When you encounter this phenomenon, then indeed you would look at it
    being of prime importance in your life in this particular moment.
It is as if it, the door has upon it emblazoned,
    "Attention, Soul, look to your Soul, enter in to the purpose!".

When it is a matte black that you are attracted to,
> that you have an affinity for, a black with no shine to it,
> > then indeed this is an indication of the lack of joy within your life.

It may only be a temporary placement in your mind,
> but, Souls, there is no temporary.

And emblazoned upon the door,
> "*Soul, attention, look to your life, look to the lack of joy!*".

Enter in, Soul, to joy.
Brighten the matte.
And we would entertain that no matter the shade of the blackness
> all are of equal importance.

When you have an attraction to grey, to grey walls, to grey attire,
> to grey accouterments, you have shut out emotions.

Emblazoned upon the door,
> "*Soul, look at what you have done!*
> *Look at how you hide from that which makes you human.*"

And enter in, Soul, to emotion, to humanity, to being, to growth.
Beloved Souls of earth, nothing is trivial.
This indeed is for your understanding.

401 Entering into the shade,
> which would be now into what is called Madonna blue,
> > this is for burn patients.

It is very soothing.
The vibration of this color soothes the pain,
> will provide an amelioration of the pain.

402 Souls of earth, we speak on the properties of brown.
Starting from the very palest, just the hint of the beige,
> the very palest can be found to be soothing
> > when placed within any room.

It may be placed as a painting, as paint, a contrast within a room.
It may be a fabric.
It may simply be a ribbon placed in the southeast corner.
Worn upon the being it will help the tension and the stress
> that you associate with any activity,
> > whether it be entering into the work,
> > whether it be entering into a competition of any kind,
> > or whether it be a speaking,

discussions with a loved one,
in all manner of activities that you individually view with tension.
It is not necessary for the activity in reality to be tense.
It is only that you view it as such.
And in those cases we would suggest the wearing
somewhere upon the body of this color
and the short meditation upon this color
before you enter in to that activity.
We would also have you know that placing the fingers thus:
thumb and forefinger touching, the two center fingers intertwined,
the left holding the right,
and the little fingers left without touching any flesh.
Holding thus, for thirty two seconds, placed in front of the solar plexus
will calm the stressor,
will calm the being.
And then, Soul, deep breath, remove the two fingers from each other
and open the thumb and forefinger.
With the color of the palest beige, the two combined,
will serendipitously engender confidence.

403 Entering in to the brown of the trees, this color is most efficacious
when placed about the child who has lost a parent.
Covering the child within this color alleviates
the desperate feeling of aloneness, of abandonment, of fear.
Within the room of this child or the sleeping area of this child,
or the bed of this child place this covering.
Place this color even upon the wall.
Place upon the wrist this color to assist this child in accepting the event.

404 Entering in to the brown of the trees, this color is most efficacious
when placed about the very old
who have become riddled with disease.

405 Entering in to the brown of the trees, this color is most efficacious
in places of institution.
We would suggest bands of this color within the room.
For it will soothe the mind and speak to the Soul and allow the being
to enter forth from this world in a semblance of comfort.
Cover the being with this color.

406 The very deepest brown shade, to almost a black brown,
>is most efficacious for those who have spinal injuries.

Placing this color upon the backs,
>sleeping upon this color, sitting with this color,
>>meditating with this color, will focus your body's
>>innate healing ability upon the disorder.

And that focus will allow the intent of altering to enter in.

407 The brown with the tinge of red
>is for those patients within institutions of mentality
>who are considered violent.

Place within your padding, Souls of earth, this color.
Upon the walls place this color.
Upon the floor place this color.
For it will speak to the Soul of this being, to the mind of this being,
>and allow rationality to enter in among the irrationality
>and the deep pain of the mind.

408 The brown with the tinge of red,
>is for those for those who have a sickness of the sea type,
>of the dizziness of altitude, even sickness of altitude.

Wearing this color, placing this color upon the pulse points of the body,
>will help to balance the mind, and therefore the body.

409 We would speak of green for the being who has cancer,
>who has been given this diagnosis.

In the preliminary stages of cancer, we suggest the muted form of green,
>the gentlest of green, the touch of new moss, worn, gazed upon,
>enveloping the being.

The stone, to hold in the palms would be chrysoprase, Soul, a light shade.
For those beings who have chosen to be chemically toxified and radiated,
>only the very deepest shade of green will be of any assistance,
>almost a black green, very dark.

The stone, at this stage, when the being is in treatment,
>must have a width and breadth and depth of at least two centimeters.

It may be larger but it may not be smaller.
For those beings who have successfully overcome the cancer,
>it would behoove the being to carry about with them for a least
>seven months beyond the lessening of the hold of the cancer,
>an emerald.

It may be in its rough state,
    that is fully acceptable.
The size is not relevant.
But it will retain for the being
    the memory of being without cancer for the body.
And so, you would carry this with you or wear that color daily.
For cancer is tenuous only in some beings.
In others, it has a tenacity.

410   Deeper into the color of green so that it is beyond the pales
      and yet not full into the spectrum of green,
        this color, Souls of earth, is soothing to burn patients
      when the burns are primarily in the lower extremities.
A covering of this shade will ease.

411   The next gradation of green, close to a forest green;
      one that you would associate with plants and trees.
This is for those beings of earth who have been told
    they have terminal illnesses,
    who have been given no hope of recovery.
This is the color of hope, Souls of earth.
This is the color that you can hold onto and know there is wellness available.
These beings in the state of emotionality or physicality
    may wear this as a blanket or as a long hooded covering
    and have the color nearby that they may gaze upon it,
    that they may touch it and hold it and enter it in to their being.
This too, should be worn in those cases,
    all through the day and all through the night.
We would place the aside that all cloth be natural fibers.
They may also, Souls of earth, drink liquids that have the green tint to them.

412   Into the farther gradation of color,
      into the very deep dark green almost into the black.
There is a depth unto the green.
This is for children attacked by ailments of cholera,
    by plague of any type, by any disease brought by insect.
Bundle the child in this color.
Place the cloth upon the child.

413   The stronger the shade of pink,
        the more vibration will enter in to the being.
Pink is particularly efficacious for those beings
        who have diseases such as the multiple sclerosis.
It would behoove any one caring for a multiple sclerotic patient,
        to place a bright pink blanket upon them.
It will, in those cases of like diseases,
        calm jittery nerves,
        and ameliorate some of the frustration felt by the beings.

414   Enter in to the color purple.
It is efficacious in the treatment of high fevers.
The placing of a purple ribbon as a band around the top of the head,
        will assist in reducing fever.
Many brain fevers that result from infection
        and from the habitation of bacteria
        will benefit from a full skull cap of purple cloth.
Silken cloth, cotton or muslin is most efficacious.
Entering in to the color of purple as the feverish child sleeps,
        will also assist in fighting the infection, the brain fever.

415   Enter in to the color purple.
The purple is of efficaciousness when applied
        to the swelling of the legs:
            gout, the swelling that occurs from burns,
            the swelling that occurs from water retention,
            the swelling that occurs from leprosy.
In those cases, warm purple cloths dipped in water
        are to be applied.

416   Enter in to the knowledge that a covering, a blanket,
        a cloak of the deepest purple when placed upon a being
        caught in the throes of great pain, of delirium,
        even unto the mental incapacities of age,
        placing this cover upon their being,
        will soothe, will calm, will provide relief.

417   We would speak on the color of red
It would behoove any who are in ill health
        to have about them that particular color.

It need not be the whole room, a simple cover, a simple pillow,
    a simple swatch, a simple painting will do.
And it will vibrate unto the wellbeing of the body.
It will set up within the cells of the body the vibration of wellness.
Take unto you into thy being that color and know wellness.

418   Yellow brings about clarity in mind and body
    when used for efficacity.
We would also suggest that each room, where sleeping or resting occurs,
    where conversation occurs, that a bit of yellow be placed.
It may be in the form of a cloth or a ribbon or a painting,
    but a bit of yellow will brighten and relax.
This is to be the yellow in the center gradation of color.

Emotions

Calm

419 It will take a while, but over time this will allow
    an easing of some of the addictive personality.
You may ease with the application of one drop lavender oil
    to be placed each time you wash the laundry.
You may also place one drop lavender at the top of the bed,
    in the corner.
The being needs soothing and calming with the addition of,
    whenever possible, involving the being with the color of lavender.
We would suggest the chamomile tea each evening after dinner.
Even in the summer heat, the chamomile made cool
    for the after dinner drink.

420 For those who have access to the kelp beds,
    especially that dark, dark green,
        we would draw your attention to the bulb.
For within the bulb are healing properties.
Open the bulb, and dip your finger in.
Place small amount, dab lightly,
    starting from the brow line down the nostril
        and under the eye and then out to the tip of the ears.
This will assist those beings who have Alzheimer,
    who are in agitation of the mind.
This may be done as often as necessary, to calm the being.

421 The stalk of the dandelion is especially efficacious
    for those beings afflicted with Alzheimer.
There is within the stalk a chemical that works
    within the convolutions of the brain of the Alzheimer patient.

It does not heal but it will calm and settle the being's angst and anger.
Three a day in the mild cases.
Six in the more moderate cases and for a severe case up to nine a day.
They are not to be cooked.
They are to be ingested as is.
You may chop them finely
> and place them upon another food that has been cooked,
> or chop them so finely that they may be placed in a liquid,
> a cool liquid, and then ingested in that manner.

Cooking will destroy the very chemical that will assist the being.

422 We bring forth the rubbing of the hand upon the forearms.
Up and down with the palm of your hand,
> up and down, up and down in a light motion,
> will soothe those beings who are troubled in mind and in body.

It is the action of the palm of your hand upon the flesh of their being that
> will draw their attention away from their confusion and their pain.

This is for those beings who are hot in a fever, caught in a coma,
> those beings who are fraught with agony due to Alzheimer
> or any like ailment of the mind.

For the fevered child this is quite soothing, Soul.
Always start with your palm upon the back of their hand,
> and then move upward unto the elbow,
> and then down again, and continue
> until they are in a restful state of being.

423 For the being in the final stages of an illness,
> it would soothe the being to have oil of roses nearby
> during the full time of their ordeal.

It will bring recall of comfort, of pleasant memories.

424 We would also have you know that the petals
> of the flower of the evening primrose
> may be used to decorate the bed of the ill.

A sprig of the evening primrose, which must be freshened each day,
> will alleviate the mal odors within a sick room,
> especially those who are closed.

It need not be a long sprig,
> but it must be at least six inches in length.

425 Souls of earth, we would speak on the color of blue.
The eggshell blue, the very lightest tinge
    of what is known as Madonna blue,
        will soothe a crying child.
Place a blanket of this color, a cloth of this color
    about the young being and it will be soothed.

426 We would ask, Soul, that to calm the mind,
    you gaze upon the color of deep indigo blue,
        for five minutes each day.
It may be in the form of material, it may be in the form of paper.
It may be in the form of glass but the color
    will assist in the calming of the mind,
        and the refocusing of the cells.

427 For those who have access to beeswax,
    we would have you understand the soothing properties of beeswax,
    a small ball of beeswax, approximately the size
    that would fit into the palm of a child's hand.
In moments of stress you would take the little ball of beeswax
    and three times roll it back and forth across the forehead
    and down the nose,
    and then back again to the forehead and down the nose.
This will prove quite soothing and relaxing.
You may also rub it upon your wrist, in the ball formation.
This, Soul, will bring soothing warmth.
It will stimulate the production of warmth in your veins,
    and it will also relax your being.

428 One drop oil of pure peppermint,
    used in the middle of the wrist lengthwise
    will assist in the first stages of pregnancy,
    for not only will the skin absorb
    but the aroma will be absorbed and will help to calm.
This may be done no more than five times during the day.

429 We speak upon the benefits of rocking.
It is no coincidence that a mother will cradle and rock the child,
    for the motion of rocking is soothing to any being.

Indeed, Souls of earth, you do not need a special chair to rock.
You may be sitting upon the ground and rock your being.
For those who are unable to rock their being
    and are confined in institutions
        or even within the home and have no control of their movement,
        then we would ask the caregiver to simulate, gently,
        the movement of rocking for the being for it will soothe
        and grant moments of peace to all beings.
Rock in a motion as you would imagine or see the waves of an ocean,
    the gentle lapping of the wave upon the shore.
That is a rhythm that will bring calm to your being.
Know there is no time element involved.
For some you may only need to rock for a minute
    and you will feel the calmness enter in.
For others greatly agitated, you may need to rock for five or ten minutes.
It will also, Souls of earth, bring you
    unto a meditative state done in a gentle motion.
It is efficacious, this rocking, for all things.
We highly recommend it for those who labor with their body,
    at the end of the day gently rock your being
    and it will soothe the pains.
For the mother who is in emotional turmoil
    and has difficulty restraining anger, temper,
    rock your being.
You may even, Souls of earth, be standing and rock your being.
Your body was designed for this ability.
All patients who are under medications need to gently rock their being.
This can be done even if no movement is able.
Gently lift the shoulders lightly,
    that is all that is needed for one who can not move.
Lift and down.
Lift and down.
Lift and down.
For those beings who are burn patients and are in the special apparatus,
    allow it to gently move in the rocking motion, soothing the being.
For those who have no caregiver available when they wish to rock,
    you may do so in your mind.
Know that your mind will soothe your being.
All you need do is rock your being within your mind.

And this technique is available to anyone,
> at any time, in any place, even unto those in coma.

Patients, those at home under severe medication,
> rock your being every hour.

To reduce the dosage of drugs for pain, rock your being every ten minutes
> and then you will not have to reach as often for the pill.

Souls of earth, this is available unto you.

430 We would speak on the properties of the frangipani flower.
Indeed, the aroma is efficaciously soothing
> to those who have within them deep wells of sorrow,
> who have within them deep wells of pain.

It is not to be wafted.
The aroma is to be inhaled
> and the inhalation held for a period of five seconds
> so that the aroma penetrates to the psyche and into the flesh.

Indeed, aromas do more than just enter in to the mind.
They do, indeed, enter in to the flesh.

431 The steam from the jasmine is most efficacious
> for those being who find themselves
> in the beginnings of those attacks
> that are called panic attacks or severe anxiety.

Place four drops jasmine oil in a quart of salted boiling water,
> to every quart of water, one tablespoon of salt.

432 This color, Madonna blue, is also for nations at war.
Is a blue that has texture and touch and thickness and the brightness.
Nations at war, covered with this color,
> will find themselves tending towards peace.

Fear

433 The lighter shades of purple, a cloak, a cloth,
> even ribbons worn about the being on the flesh, not within the hair,
> will give courage to beings who have let fear rule their lives.

It will grant them peace
> so that they may move forward with confidence.

434 For the child who has great fears of new experiences,
> who clings out of fear.

Sit opposite the child, place your hands out, palm up,
> and then, Soul, bring them in
>> and hold them against the area between the heart and the navel,
>> and ask the child to do the same.

Hold this position for as long as the child is comfortable,
> and then slowly move your hands away.

Ask the child to do this once more,
> and then ask the child how they feel.

And when they respond that they are comforted, that they feel good,
> you may inform the child
>> that at any time they begin to feel again that fear,
>> they need only place their hand once upon that area,
>> and they will be helped in overcoming their anxiety.

435 We would have you understand that the kidneys
> are holders of anger in many cases.

Both the stomach and the kidneys hold anger.
And we say to release the anger, give it to Creator.
Creator will gladly accept the Energy for then He can alter it.
You have, Soul, worry that you hold within.
And we would ask that you offer that also.
And understand that worry gnaws at your vitals,
> eats at them, debilitates them all.

The body is finite and emotions are an integral part
> of the operation of the machinery of the body.

Stress, tension, anxiety, worry.
Souls of earth, you do such damage
> to this most blessed being you call body.

Accept[35] and then there is no need to constantly overcome the anger,
> the worry, the tension, the stress.

Know you have purpose.

436 Many have yet to understand the physical consequences
> of excess emotionality, of negative emotionality.

Your mind, the seat of your emotions, is not separate from the body.
Indeed, your mind and body are one.
You can not separate the reaction of the emotions upon your being.

---

35 accept - to be in a state of knowing all is a lesson
and has reason for being.

The kidneys act within the body as a cleanser,
>   much as your water is cleansed through various modalities
>   of toxins and poisons to some extent.

Your kidneys were designed to assist your body
>   in decomposing and filtering toxins.

And, Souls of earth, you overwhelm this generous organ of your being
>   so that it is unable to be effective.

And you overwhelm this organ
>   by the ingestion of polluted nutrients, indeed,
>   but also by the pollution of negativity emotionality.

The anger that roils within your being,
>   do you think that the energy of this anger automatically dissipates?

Soul, it must have some place to go.

And the body is the recipient of the consequences of anger.

And the kidneys valiantly attempt to rid the body of the excess toxins.

Stress is detrimental to thy being.

It causes an excess of chemicals and disturbs the balance of your body
>   and again the valiant kidneys are called upon to assist
>   in cleansing the body and removing that which should not be.

A kidney cleanse is in order to bring back balance.

We would recommend three days purified water, clear broth,
>   vegetable broth only, no caffeine, no sugars, not even a fruit juice.

This will enable the kidney to heal, for no stress will be placed upon it.

And it will be brought back unto its healthy state.

437 Healing and releasing the holding of fear emotion.

Sitting with feet together, place arms out with hands up,
>   having elbows bent in a receiving position.

Then allow the green turquoise color to enter in to
>   all aspects of your being.

When your fingertips start to tingle
>   and you may feel the Energy start to be heavy feeling in the arms,
>   then form golden Energy balls in each palm.

As the Energy grows and gets heavy, start to move the two hands together
>   with the sides touching, forming a bowl.

As this is happening,
>   the two golden balls come together as one golden Energy ball.

When the one golden Energy ball is made,
>   slowly bring the ball to the center eye
>   and allow the Energy from that golden ball
>   to enter in unto all parts of being.

In the receiving of Energy,
> do not be alarmed if you feel shaking in any part of your being.

When the golden Energy has been absorbed from the hands,
> then you may move your hands back to the receiving position
> > in front of you with the elbows bent, palms up.

Now receive as on a glorious sunny day the color of sky blue.
Allow this color to permeate all parts of your being.

438 The awakening after a short period of sleep is, in general,
> and we speak loosely in general only, due to a physical causation,
> > an interruption of the blood flow to a part of the body.

It is your autonomic alarm as it were, for you to awaken and thrash about.
This generally brings a relieve to that particularly affected body part.
It may be inners or outers.
The inability to fall asleep, to fall into a restful sleep,
> is related to the inability to still the mind.

It is, in some cases, a physical relationship
> and these may be discovered within the medical community.

There is a fear associated with the stilling of the mind.
It is a buried fear but it affects most drastically,
> not only in the inability to sleep,
> > but in the ability to restore the body and to rest the mind.

It is a reactionary fear to the lifetime that the Soul is in.
It is a way of attempting to destroy the body and the mind.
It is from fear, the basic fear.
The source is always the same, the inability to accept the life one is in.
And is a serious attempt to avoid their purpose,
> for it is difficult to function in a debilitated state
> > one that has not been agreed to as part of a karmic relationship,
> > but is instead a Soul choice altered by the lack of acceptance.

439 We would have you understand the strain
> you place upon your being with the concept of worry.

Worrying, Souls of earth, is detrimental to the physical,
> emotional and mental well being of your body.

It is an imbalance, physically, emotionally and mentally.
Worrying affects the inners of your being.
It affects the actual flow of energy within your being.
It parts the energy that would flow in a smooth manner,
> divides the energy so that the flow is interrupted.

And this places stress and strain upon all of your being.
Worrying is not conducive to optimum balance.
It is not conducive to clear thought.
It is not conducive to healing.
It, in fact, is disruptive when a being is attempting to heal.
Understand, Souls, the worry about self affects self,
    and worry about another affects the other also,
        for you are sending energy that is parted to that being.
You are not sending a flow of Energy.
Worry serves no purpose except as a lesson to overcome, to learn from,
    to cease this practice that is detrimental to your well being
    or the well being of another.
Understand, it disrupts the very physicality of your being;
    the mind disconnects from the triad of wellness.
Worry can lead to being distraught.
Distraught places more stress upon your brain process,
    your emotional process, and your physical.
It helps to balance your being when you are in the mode of compassion,
    in the mode of worry, you unbalance.

Appendix A
*Daily East Ritual**

"East: it is the passageway to the Farside through the eye.
Its Truth is to be understood as a Love by humanity.
Focus on east at dawn, allowing the negativity
      to flow from your being,
         receiving unto yourself the goodness of Creator.
All humanity has the availability of this pathway.
The ritual of the east is the Soul's own response
      to the positive east which is tao.
Face east, two minutes.
Look with the eyes to the horizon's level.
In the brick wall or the iron cage, or the ornate boardwalk,
      know that the east will be with your Soul.
Turn clockwise once to heal.
Energy will flow to the matter before it.
All organs of the body are healed in the circle turn."

*Creator Trilogy, <u>Energy From The Source</u>, Appendix A

Appendix B
Book List

Published

by Lucy Dumouchelle

The Binary
*The Mend (Holistic Healing
Through Channelled Entities)*

by Kitty Lloyd

Creator Trilogy
First Key   Energy From The Source
Second Key   So Shall It Be
Third Key   Until Then

Forthcoming

by Lucy Dumouchelle

The Binary
*Holistic Healing Through
Channelled Ancients*
Healing From The Farside

Creator Trilogy
Healing With Echo
Healing With Value
Healing With Intent

by Kitty Lloyd

Creator Trilogy
Trilogy of Consciousness
The Gathering Time
From Whence It Came
Ecstasy

Creator Trilogy
Supreme Being Trilogy
How To Step To The Path
Angels' Ecstasy
The Rejoicing

Creator Trilogy
Echo
Value
Keepers Of The Light

Published through Mountaintop Healing Publishing Inc

www.ingramcontent.com/pod-product-compliance
Lightning Source LLC
Chambersburg PA
CBHW081345040426
42450CB00015B/3309